THE LEARNING DISABLED CHILD

A SCHOOL AND FAMILY CONCERN

J. JEFFRIES MC WHIRTER

RESEARCH PRESS COMPANY

2612 NORTH MATTIS AVENUE
CHAMPAIGN, ILLINOIS 61820

*This book is dedicated to the memory of
Clara Minden Plasker,
a wise and valiant woman,
who showed compassion, love, and warmth
to children with special problems,
and to her grandson,
Paul John.*

Contents

Foreword

I might as well get my anxieties and my enthusiasms expressed in these first two paragraphs. When asked to write this foreword, I protested since I am not a specialist in the field covered by this book. The reply was that "you're a psychologist of long standing and you've written in a number of areas in psychology. I'm sure this won't be a difficult task for you. I'd really *like* to have your viewpoint of the book in the form of a foreword." Well, Jeff McWhirter is persuasive and I like him, so I said "yes" but with misgivings. But *after* reading the manuscript of the book, my anxiety was greatly reduced. I think I understand what he is writing about and can comment upon the book without loss of professional self-respect.

To describe my enthusiasm for the book will make clear why I could write the preceding sentence. Over the past fifty some years, I have been a reader and an editor of many hundreds of professional books and journal manuscripts; this particular piece of writing is among the best organized and clearly written manuscripts of any that I have read—perhaps among the best twenty or twenty-five. It is so well done that I feel sufficiently rewarded for the time involved because of what I have learned.

One of the first things the reader should understand is that McWhirter has a remarkable set of competencies for writing this book. He addresses it to parents, teachers, and counselors. He is all three. Beyond this he is of course a psychologist with much cognitive understanding of the field and considerable experience as a psychological consultant of teachers. His distinctive strength, however, lies in the fact that he is a parent of two boys who have learning disabilities which he and his wife, Mary, another sensitive and perceptive person, have *lived* with over the years. They *know* what can be done by parents in collaboration with teachers and learning disability specialists.

I suggest that after the reader completes Chapter 1 that he turn next to the Epilogue. These two sections are about the two sons, Bob and Mark; they are also "before" and "after" sections. Anyone reading them will feel greatly encouraged about what can be done, what *has* been done. He or she will be ready to read the rest of the book to find out the causes and the "how" of dealing with learning disabilities.

It should be clearly stated, however, that bringing these two sons so intimately into the book is no source of embarrassment to them; their privacy has not been invaded. In fact only a few days ago, Mark said proudly to me, "You know, Daddy has written a book about Bob and me." Nor is there any embarrassment drawn by the other three children who have no such problems. They accept their brothers' problems with understanding and helpfulness. Bob and Mark are cheerful and socially integrated with little to suggest the difficulties they have had and, to some degree, will continue to have.

The organization of the book and the sequence of chapters is clearly defensible. An examination of the Table of Contents and a reading of the author's Preface point up that the learning disabilities so apparent in school and home and the sensory deficiencies which are the primary cause of any disability are to be given first place. These must be understood before anything else is provided. The emotional behavior so often accompanying the child's sense of frustration in school is next considered but only *after* the basic physiological causes are understood. Chapter 9 is a favorite of mine because I am a counseling psychologist who is particularly sensitive to the emotions and self-perceptions of people, but this chapter and the three following it come at the right place. They should not have been introduced earlier.

All of Part II was rewarding to me because so much is presented in the way of specific procedures that *both* parents and teachers can use to help the child meet his emotional needs and thereby modify his behavior. Any parent or teacher can find applications of the Premack Principle (Chapter 13) that will open up a new world for the child but again "the price is right"; this chapter comes after the more basic behavior principles proposed in Chapter 12.

The eclectic position of the author is described in the Introduction to Part II. McWhirter is not a "one-school-of-thought" psychologist; he is a "find-the-best-procedure-for-each-child" psychologist. He suggests that teacher or parent adapt the strategy to the particular child-in-situation and to the practitioner's feeling of comfort with the strategy, not adapt all children and all strategies to one psychological school of thought. I like this approach. It provides the richest reservoir of aids to children. McWhirter writes like a psychologist who has dealt intimately with children and parents and teachers as they *are*, not like a writer who deals primarily with ideas *about* children, parents, and teachers.

One basic theme of the book is that home and parents are vitally important even though the disability may appear most vividly in the school. In fact the parent can do a great deal for the emotional life of the child even when little is done in the school to meet the basic learning needs. Neither teacher nor parent can place full responsibility for remediation on the other. Unless both school and home understand causes and strategies for ameliorating the child's weaknesses and frustration, full remediation is impossible. This is where the school counselor or psychologist may contribute a great deal by serving as consultant in the school-home, teacher-parent relationship. This is the thrust of Part III of the book although the strategies for the parent are suggested in all preceding chapters as well. This is really a book for parents directly as well as for teachers and for the home-school relationship.

The concepts and strategies of this book, when applied, will bring an easing of frustration and an increase in self-esteem into the lives of children who are in learning trouble. It will bring light and hope into the lives of parents and teachers as well because there are things to *do*, tested strategies that they can employ. Children with learning disabilities have heartaches but so do the parents and teachers who are committed to them. An eventual easing of heartaches is perhaps the major outcome of this book.

C. Gilbert Wrenn

Preface

I first thought of writing this book while driving across country from Maine to Arizona. I had finished a visiting summer appointment at the University of Maine at Orono and to get back on time for classes at Arizona State University, we drove through the night. The children were asleep in the back of the van. As we drove those long hours through Pennsylvania, Indiana, Missouri, Oklahoma, Mary and I talked. The shape of this volume took form. I have tried to do three things in this book: first, to make a very personal statement about learning disabilities both to parents and to professionals; second, to provide a relatively clear explanation of educational and psychological theories that have had some meaning to parents and professionals; and third, to provide some practical, concrete ways of helping children at home and school. I hope I have succeeded.

The book has been written for three audiences: parents, teachers and teachers-in-training, and school support personnel usually classified under pupil personnel services.

Parents. Parents need information about their learning disabled child and his educational and psychological problems. Parents have the potential to reinforce school learning and help in the child's development with activities, games, and involvement at home. Parents can and should be helped to provide an extension of the school's program.

Teachers. Both regular and special classroom teachers need information about educational and psychological strategies for special students. The exercises are provided for the teacher to use as a supplement to the remedial program. The psychological strategies should prove helpful in structuring the classroom more appropriately.

Support Personnel. Counselors, psychologists, and social workers need information about teaching approaches and psychological structures as they work with children, teachers, and parents. This book is intended to provide a resource for the helping person in his work with families.

The book is divided into three sections. Part I focuses on educational concerns and problems. A description of learning disabilities of the three sensory modalities is provided along with material, procedures, and games which may be useful to parents and teachers. Part II deals with practical and concrete psychological information. Part III is written primarily for professionals with the intent of bringing the school and home in closer alliance. This section contains information which could help the counselor or psychologist fulfill the consultant role.

I want to thank C. Gilbert Wrenn, Professor Emeritus, Arizona State University. Professor Wrenn has been a consistently supportive colleague and a caring friend. This book has been a family project, not only in the content but in the process as well. I would like to thank Mary, my best friend and wife, who typed the manuscript several times, who corrected copy, who was there for discussion, and whose idea it was in the first place. In many ways she is as much the author as I am.

And I would like to thank our children: Bob, Ben, Anna, Mark, and Paula who
    washed the windows,
    fixed the cupboards,
    cooked the dinner,
    vacuumed the floors,
    made the beds
so Mom could type and Dad could write. They are the ones who make it all worthwhile.

PART I

EDUCATIONAL PERSPECTIVES

During the past five years there has been a burgeoning of educational techniques that are important to the learning disabled child, his teachers, and his parents. Specifically, educational techniques and materials have been introduced at a staggering rate. Diagnostic methods for identifying the manifestations of learning disabilities have become much more precise.

This section deals with some of these developments. Teachers and parents alike need to be more aware of the phenomena of learning disabilities. Teachers should know so that they can respond with appropriate alternatives and options to help the child learn *and* feel better about himself. Parents need this information so that they can put into perspective the problems with which they must live and so that they can be partners with school personnel in the teaching process.

The content of several of the chapters provides basic information as it relates to learning disabilities. In addition to the theory which forms the basis for these chapters, I

1

have included experiential exercises where they are feasible. Hopefully, these experiences will allow the reader to understand as well as to know. Chapters 1 and 2 present some of the confusion and facts surrounding the area of learning disabilities. A learning process model which relates the learning functions with the sense modalities also is included. Chapter 3 provides a general overview of systems of educational theory for the remediation of learning problems. Chapters 4, 6, and 8 discuss specific learning disabilities with an attempt to delineate discrete areas of concern.

Several chapters provide activities for various classifications of problems. These activities were selected because of their usefulness to teachers and parents in helping the learning disabled child with his deficit. They were selected also because of their potential for enjoyment. Many of the games and activities in Chapters 5, 7, and 8 are what teachers call motivational devices. They provide the child incentives to further and continue learning. At home and at school they should be used as a supplement to basic educational programs. They should not be viewed as a substitution for a strong school program which consistently evaluates and re-evaluates the specific learning deficits and strengths and responds to both deficits and strengths with appropriate instruction.

1

Confusions Related to Learning Disabilities

The Story of Robert, a Learning Disabled Child

I would like you to picture the following scene which actually happened to a learning disabled child whom I know and with whom I have worked. It is likely that some of you reading this book either have or teach a learning disabled child and will be reminded of events in the life of this particular child.

Robert was five and starting kindergarten. He seemed to be bright, cheerful, and looking forward to school. After he started school, he did enjoy going. Being of an independent nature, he never wanted to stay home. He didn't want his mom to walk him the five or six blocks to school, and in the first few weeks he discovered several different routes to and from school. At supper in the evening, he would chatter away in some detail about the events which happened on the way to and from school. Since independence and verbal behavior are potential

3

indicators of intelligence, Robert demonstrated to his parents that he was capable and bright. Indications were that he had at least average, and probably above-average, I.Q.

Then trouble started. The first incident was in learning to tie his shoestrings. Because Robert was a first-born child and because a brother and sister had followed closely behind him, his mother was rushed and hadn't bothered trying to teach him to tie a bow. It was easier and quicker to tie it for him and then go on to the thousand-and-one tasks which had to be done. Shortly before conference time, the teacher sent a note home, "Robert cannot tie his own shoestrings." At the first conference the parents were faced with a bulletin board with silhouettes of paper shoes with string ties. Robert did not have his shoe displayed because he still couldn't tie a bow. To themselves the parents explained away this apparent problem on Robert's lack of development of small-muscle coordination.

Another incident occurred later in the year. The kindergarten class was working on telephone and street numbers. Robert was having a frustrating time. He couldn't seem to grasp this relatively simple task. His parents, still expecting above-average performance, began to have doubts about his intellectual ability and began to vacillate between, "He's bright but just doesn't try hard enough" to "He's really slow and we're just fooling ourselves about his brightness" to "He really is bright and actually knows his address and phone number but is using his 'dumbness' to bug the teacher because he feels that she doesn't like him."

Robert's performance that first year continued to be marginal and inconsistent. In fact, it was poor enough that his parents decided to hold off his entrance into first grade for a year because they felt perhaps he was not develop-mentally ready for school.

A year later Robert began first grade. The problems continued. His teacher, a marvelous and dedicated person,

4

spent additional time working with him, but he still didn't appear to be learning adequately. That spring his parents had him tested by a psychologist. The results indicated he was above average on comprehension, information, and responsibility, but considerably below average on some of the other subtests, particularly coding. The psychologist suggested that it was just a phase that Robert would probably outgrow.

Robert continued doing increasingly poor work in school and fell farther behind. He seemed to alternate years between a good teacher who was understanding, flexible, and interested to a rigid, unaccepting, and critical teacher the following year. His attitude, willingness to try, and motivation were, of course, greatly affected by the teacher's response. He became more argumentative, obnoxious, and negative about school. His self-concept began to suffer with his growing awareness of his lack of "normalness." However, no one seemed to be able to define the problem, and no one seemed to know what to do.

Three years later Robert was diagnosed by another psychologist as learning disabled with specific problems in visual perception, auditory perception, and auditory memory. That diagnosis became a turning point and things began to improve. The problems in learning began to make sense. Remedial procedures which were implemented helped Robert, particularly in learning to read. His parents involved him at home in activities which seemed potentially helpful in his development. His improved social behaviors reflected the awareness of his problem and the procedures used to help.

Perhaps you can see something of yourself or of your learning disabled child in this story. It is really not too untypical of the history of many learning disabled children and their parents. Throughout this book, I would like to speak to you from two points of view. The first viewpoint is as a counseling psychologist who works with learning disabled children and their parents and the second is as the parent of a learning disabled child. Robert in the preceding story is my son.

Frustrations and Confusion
Experiential Knowledge

Any parent of a learning disabled child knows the frustration and confusion surrounding the term "learning disability." These parents know the frustration and confusion because of the inconsistent behavior of their child. They know the frustration because they possibly have heard neighborhood children, in the sometimes cruel manner of youngsters, call out in reference to their child, "Hey, Retard!" They know the confusion and frustration because they have experienced the school counselor or psychologist trying to explain why their child was not doing well in certain school subjects. They know the confusion because of their own difficulty when they try to explain to friends and relatives the problems their child faces.

The teacher of the learning disabled child also understands the confusion and if sensitive to the needs of parents and children, he also appreciates the frustrations.

Multiplicity of Professional Disciplines and Approaches

In part, this confusion arises from the multiplicity of professional disciplines and theoretical approaches involved in handling learning disabilities. Significant manifestations of the confusion from such multiplicity are diverse terminology and many differences in designating etiology (cause), making diagnoses, and treating the children.

Profusion of Terms. More than 40 English terms have been used in the professional literature which could apply to this group of children.

In a selected review of the literature the author found numerous terms used to describe or distinguish learning

disabled children. A partial list follows:
    learning disabilities
    aggressive behavior disorder
    attention disorder
    brain dysfunction
    brain injured
    cerebral dysfunction
    character impulse disorder
    clumsy child syndrome
    conceptually handicapped
    diffuse brain damage
    disorders of impulse control
    disorders of motor coordination
    disorders of perception
    dyslexic
    hyperkinetic behavior disorder
    hyperkinetic impulse syndrome
    mild neurosatory deficit
    minimal brain dysfunction
    minimal brain injury
    minimal cerebral damage
    minimal cerebral dysfunction
    minimal cerebral injury
    minimal chronic brain damage syndrome
    minor brain damage
    neurologically handicapped
    neurophrenia
    organic behavior disorder
    organic brain damage
    perceptually impaired
    perceptually handicapped
    psychoneurological learning disorders
    specific learning disabilities
    visual-motor perceptual lag
    The above list is not complete and does not represent all the possibilities which exist. The list does illustrate part of the reason for the confusion. A child with a learning disability may be labeled with any one of these terms,

depending on the academic discipline of the professional who diagnosed him, the particular orientation of that professional, and the state in which the family resides. This problem is even more acute when one considers that 23 different states use different legal terms to describe the learning disabled child. The problems that this represents can be graphically and hypothetically experienced by imagining that you have a learning disabled child and that you move a great deal; your child will be known by a different term as he moves into those 23 states. The "learning disabled/emotionally disturbed" child in Arizona becomes "neurologically handicapped" when his family moves across the state line.

As earlier noted, part of the reason for the proliferation of terms in this area is due to the fact that professionals from *different* disciplines have been associated with learning disabled children. These professionals include physicians such as pediatricians, neurologists, and psychiatrists. Their orientation has frequently been to focus on brain function, genetics, and behavior relating to etiological factors. Psychologists, who also work with these children, frequently have viewed them from the perspective of their psychic functions including interpersonal and intrapersonal data. Optometrists too work with learning disabled children. As might be expected, they tend to emphasize the ocular activity of the children. Finally, both general and special educators are involved and are concerned primarily with instruction and remediation.

The potential benefits of multidisciplinary approaches promise much in understanding and educating the learning disabled child. The fact remains, however, that at present the multiplicity of the academic disciplines involved has created confusion in the number of terms used to describe the problem.

Diversity in Etiology, Diagnoses, and Treatment. The backgrounds of professionals involved create even more problems of diversity than those relating to terminology.

Unfortunately, professionals frequently don't agree on the etiology, diagnosis, or method of treatment for learning disabilities.

It is true that often we are dealing with theories and not with facts. We frequently don't know how the problem occurs or what physiological mechanisms or psychological factors are involved. Etiology continues to be an unsolved riddle. Several writers and a number of studies (Drew, 1956; Hermann, 1959) suggest that learning disability has a hereditary basis. Apparently there are families in which the disorder seems to be transmitted genetically. Relatives on either or both sides of the family may have had similar problems, and it is assumed that the child's learning disability is inherited.

Pre-natal conditions too are often thought to contribute to learning disabilities. Nutritional problems of the expectant mother, such as protein deficiency, are sometimes suspected to be factors contributing to learning problems. Excessive bleeding and overexposure to radiation, including X-rays, also have been considered factors. Another suspected cause is infectious diseases, such as measles.

Birth problems, such as premature birth, frequently are considered the cause of the learning disability. We do know that prolonged inadequate oxygen supply to the brain can cause brain damage. Evidence exists which suggests that in some cases the learning disability, usually referred to as minimal cerebral dysfunction, may have resulted from a similar problem. It is a fact that most learning disabled children are first-borns. This fact may be related to the mother's longer labors and the resultant complications.

Learning disabilities sometimes are attributed to post birth problems. High fevers and/or seizures sometimes appear to contribute to later learning difficulty. Infectious diseases which cause damage to the central nervous system, such as meningitis and encephalitis, also may be related to learning disorders.

In addition to assigning an etiological reason for the problem, there is difficulty in discovering the etiological basis of the learning disability. Many have felt the inability to read, write, spell correctly, and put numbers in their correct sequence was symptomatic of visual difficulties. A recent theory blames such learning disability problems on those functions of the inner ear that control equilibrium. Another theory is that learning disabilities are caused by a disturbance in the neuro-chemical system of the brain.

Diagnosis at present too often is based on superficial observation which does not lead to adequate understanding or effective remedial techniques.

Much of the confusion in understanding learning disability as it relates to a particular child is due to the attempt to make the concept a global problem. This leads to different beliefs of what the global problem is and what might be effective in its treatment. Many writers (Kirk, 1972; Wallace and Kaufman, 1973; McCarthy and McCarthy, 1969) suggest that we must begin to concentrate on specific deficits rather than global factors and utilize this data for better understanding and for the development of prescriptive teaching. We must relate the technique to the needs of the individual child.

Inconsistency in Behavior

Closely related to the preceding discussion are the frustration and confusion which surround the actual behavior of the learning disabled child. The frustration and confusion are rooted in the inconsistency of the child's behavior. In fact, the most consistent thing about a learning disabled child is the inconsistency which he is likely to exhibit in his behavior. The behaviors and problems which typify one learning disabled child may be totally different from the behaviors and problems of another learning disabled child. In some instances even the problem behavior of one child may not be consistent. A learning disabled child who reverses words sometimes sees the word *was* as *saw* and yet at other times reads *was* as *was*. Needless to say, this inconsistency is a frustrating thing for the parent, teacher, and the child himself.

To get personal again, when my son began school, our knowledge of his learning problem also began. Part of our frustration as parents and his frustration as a learning disabled child was his inconsistency. For example, he would follow directions and complete tasks at home. At school he would not do his work adequately and appeared not to follow directions. Consequently, he appeared to be very inconsistent in terms of cooperation. Another example is related to reading. He was frustrated with learning to read and developed a disinterest in reading. Yet he liked to discuss ideas and concepts. His interest patterns were inconsistent with the difficulty which he was experiencing. Finally, he was unable to manipulate small objects, had problems with his balance, and frequently seemed clumsy. Despite this, Robert was an extremely agile and graceful climber. His demonstrating these incongruous behaviors did not seem reasonable and indeed confused and frustrated us. Again, those of you reading this book who are parents of a learning disabled child may recognize some of these same confusions and frustrations in your own child and in yourselves.

Parents as a Source of Confusion and Frustration

Another source of confusion which relates to learning disabilities exists within the parents themselves. Frequently this confusion arises from a lack of understanding of their child's learning problem and the inability to get good, clear, definitive information. The problem is compounded further by the feelings which arise from the frustration of being the parent of a learning disabled child. This last point is critical to effective parenting. It is my belief that increased understanding of the specific learning disability can lead to deliberate modification of interaction patterns. Two ways in which this understanding can help are related to feelings of anxiety and guilt which the parents may experience.

Lowering Anxiety. First, increased understanding can help lower the anxiety which most parents feel when their children are not doing as well as expected. By recognizing the problem as a physical and educational one that can be greatly helped by adequate educational and instructional programming, the parent can focus more on here-and-now issues and be less concerned about future problems. The situation goes something like this: Junior doesn't take out the garbage when he is supposed to and, perhaps, even after he has been asked. Mother is annoyed, angry, and frustrated. Besides being upset about the garbage, she also says to herself, "If I can't get him to do his chores even when I remind him about them, how is he ever going to do well in high school or college? How can he ever hold down a job?" By recognizing the interface of the learning disability with the behavioral problem, mother may be able to deal more appropriately with the misbehavior. Her anxiety with future concerns is minimized.

Alleviating Guilt. Second, increased understanding can help alleviate the inappropriate feeling of guilt. Most people know what really terrible parents they are anyway. When one has a youngster with special problems, the parent frequently assumes that if he had done things differently, this problem wouldn't exist. The individual often says to himself, "If I had just been more strict, or more lenient, or more rigid, or more flexible, then my child wouldn't be having this trouble with his learning and with his behavior." Besides being one of the most useless commodities around (Bettelheim, 1950), guilt too frequently serves as an immobilizer. It is as if the parent feels so guilty about having gotten the child into this fix that she feels she will mess up again, even if she adopts a new behavior toward the child. She says then, "I can't stand to feel any more guilt, so I'm not going to change my behavior." By recognizing the source of the learning

12

disability, parents can relieve themselves of some of the negative emotion which they frequently experience and exhibit and which interferes with their interaction with their child.

I am obviously not arguing for *not changing* behavior. I am arguing for changing the inappropriate feelings which limit healthy interaction. I am arguing mostly for parents to take some of the pressure off themselves since pressure almost always gets transferred directly or indirectly to the child. *I am arguing for parents to take off the pressure in order to let their common sense help guide their relationship with the child.*

Altering Parental Reactions. Another way increased knowledge of learning disabilities can help is more substantive. By recognizing the behavioral correlates of a specific learning disability the parent and the teacher may better anticipate the child's reaction to a specific situation *and can modify their own behavior accordingly.* Let's take a specific example. Your child has problems of auditory reception and integration. The child suffers a disability in the intake and integration of information obtained through hearing. This is frequently expressed as an auditory perception or as an auditory memory problem. Once the parent and the teacher fully accept this disability as a problem, then the adult can modify the way he responds to the child. By taking the specific learning disability into account, the adult can modify her behavior to best facilitate the growth of the child. Subsequent chapters will focus on ways in which this may be accomplished.

2

Learning Disabilities and the Learning Process

Interrelationship of Child, School, and Family

There is an unavoidable interrelationship of influence and responsibility among the child, school, and family.

It is an accepted fact that an individual's behavior and attitudes are markedly affected by his family and by his school. The family, particularly the parents, exert a tremendous influence upon the socialization of the child. The school, especially the teacher, continues the socialization process. The parents' attitudes, beliefs, and knowledge are critical in the child's formation of self-concept and in his subsequent achievement in school and life. Concomitantly, the teacher's involvement also affects the child's belief about himself.

At the same time the child affects both the teacher and family. This is particularly true of a child with learning disabilities. The family of such a child frequently bears the brunt of the behavioral problems which arise from the learning disabilities. They must face the consequences of the child's difficulties in learning. The family, especially the parents, must cope with what these behavioral and educational problems mean in terms of their daily routine. They face the need to spend extra time and effort to deal with these problems.

Parents want to do a good job of parenting; they desire happiness, success, and useful, productive lives for their children. They are most concerned about the unmet needs of their children. Many parents of learning disabled children therefore are frustrated. Some are frightened. Much of this frustration and fear stems from a lack of knowledge of learning disabilities and/or from a lack of knowledge about what to do with and for their children. Given the basic knowledge of learning disabilities and the problems which arise from this area, parents can learn to be more effective in their interactions with their learning disabled child. They can develop a relationship which will increase the child's competence and self-esteem.

The teacher also is affected by the needs of the learning disabled child. The normal school problems with which she must cope are greatly expanded. She must deal with the challenge of a child who is frequently frustrated by his inability to learn and therefore disruptive in class. With large classes and limited resources, the teacher often is frustrated by her own limitations in meeting the child's needs. She is caught in a dilemma.

Yet, teachers can improve the climate within the classroom if they have more knowledge of psychological and educational procedures relating to the disabled child. They can structure their own interaction with the child more helpfully. With greater understanding of the problem, they are in a better position to help the disabled child.

Believing, then, that both parents and teachers can be more effective if they have more information about the child and his difficulty, we will turn our attention to defining what learning disabilities are and how they affect the learning process.

Two Definitions of Learning Disabilities

One aid in understanding the concept of learning disabilities is the use of definitions. Consequently, two definitions are presented: one by two leaders in the field, Kirk and Bateman (1962); the other, by the National Advisory Committee on Handicapped Children (1968). Kirk and Bateman (1962) state:

A learning disability refers to a retardation, disorder, or delayed development in one or more of the processes of speech, language, reading, writing, arithmetic, or other school subjects resulting from a psychological handicap caused by a possible cerebral dysfunction and/or emotional or behavior disturbances. It is not the result of mental retardation, sensory deprivation, or cultural or instructional factors. [Reprinted with permission. Kirk, S.A., and Bateman, B. Diagnosis and remediation of learning disabilities. *Exceptional Children*, 29:2, 1962, p. 73.]

The National Advisory Committee on Handicapped Children (1968) offered the following:

A learning disability refers to one or more significant deficits in essential learning processes requiring special educational techniques for its remediation.

Children with learning disability generally demonstrate a discrepancy between expected and actual achievement in one or more areas, such as spoken, read, or written language, mathematics, and spatial orientation.

The learning disability referred to is not primarily the result of sensory, motor, intellectual, or emotional handicap, or lack of opportunity to learn.

Deficits are to be defined in terms of accepted diagnostic procedures in education and psychology.

Essential learning processes are those currently referred to in behavior science as perception, integration, and expression, either verbal or nonverbal.

Special education techniques for remediation require educational planning based on the diagnostic procedures and findings. [Reprinted with permission. National Advisory Committee on Handicapped Children. *Special Education for Handicapped Children*, First Annual Report. Washington, D.C.: U.S. Department of Health, Education, and Welfare, Office of Education, Jan. 31, 1968, p. 34.]

Common Clauses of These Definitions

These definitions as well as others which have been proposed include three common concepts. First, they include an *intact clause* which requires "adequate" intellectual ability with freedom from gross impairment of basic sensory organs, freedom from the effects of culturally disadvantaged circumstances, and freedom from emotional disturbance. Second, the definitions include a *discrepancy clause* which requires a significant difference between the actual academic achievement of the child and his potential academic achievement. Third, they contain an *exclusion clause* which helps delineate the learning disability by mentioning those categories of children already excluded. Of course, these clauses are interrelated as the following elaboration will reflect.

One way of defining a concept is to determine what it is *not*. The definitions agree that learning disabilities are *not* the result of mental retardation, sensory deprivation, cultural differences, or instructional factors.

A learning disability is not mental retardation. Although the problem of defining mental retardation is itself a complicated issue, a recent definition (Heber, 1961) formulated by the American Association on Mental Deficiency states, "Mental retardation refers to *subaverage general intellectual* functioning which originates during the developmental period and is associated with impairment in adaptive behavior" (italics added) (p. 499). Learning disabled children are *not* considered to be of "subaverage general intelligence." In fact, by definition the child must possess average or above-average intellectual ability to be considered learning disabled.

A learning disability is not sensory deprivation. Sensory deprivation refers to problems in learning which are the result of subtle but permanent alterations in the central nervous system because of severe early limitation of sensory stimulus. Learning disabled children are not considered to have been deprived of sensory stimulation during earlier developmental periods.

A learning disability is not due to cultural or educational factors. Some youngsters have difficulty learning specific school subjects because of cultural factors. For instance, children may have difficulty with language functions because they are raised in a culture where English is a second language. Obviously such children may have difficulty in schools where allowances for this are not made. However, these children are not considered to be learning disabled; neither are youngsters who have difficulty in other specific areas attributable to poor instruction.

Indeed, the problems of these youngsters—the mentally retarded, the sensory deprived, and the educationally disadvantaged—are serious, and the solutions require understanding, commitment, and specific educational approaches. The point is, however, that children with learning and behavior problems stemming from the preceding factors are not considered to be learning disabled.

Elaboration of the Definitions

After looking at what a learning disability is not, let us turn to what a learning disability is. The definitions already provided agree that a learning disability is a delayed development in the essential learning processes. That is, either the receptive, the integrative, or the expressive abilities of the learning disabled child develop more slowly than those of the normal or average child. These problems result in a discrepancy in the actual achievement of the child and in what one would expect the child to learn, given his intelligence and the absence of more obvious problems. The areas which are usually of most concern are those of spoken and written language primarily because those areas affect subjects that are critical to school-related success, i.e., reading, arithmetic, and spatial relationships.

Essentially, the term learning disability is a blanket label used to describe a variety of behaviors. The term includes youngsters with so-called minimal brain dysfunction (MBD), but it also includes children whose behavior and learning performances are discrepant but who do not demonstrate hard signs of neurological involvement. The presence of a neurological dysfunction is inferred from "soft" or marginal behavioral characteristics. Learning disabilities are essentially the result of perceptual problems which stem from the neurological system.

Areas of Disability in the Learning Process

Although the neurological mechanism by which distortions of perception occur is not fully understood, most scholars in the field postulate that perceptual problems find their expression in three distinct but interrelated realms: receptive (or input) functions, integrative functions, and expressive (or output) functions. Figure 1 shows these functions. It must be recognized that in fact the person operates in a unified consistent manner with these functions. That is, both psychologically and physiologically, these functions operate in extremely close harmony. Unfortunately, any diagram which separates the areas of functioning as if there were independent functions obscures the basic interdependence of the three functions. Recognizing this as a problem however, we can divide the learning process into three interrelated components: receptive (or input) abilities; integrative abilities; and expressive (or output) abilities.

Figure 1 Components of the Learning Process

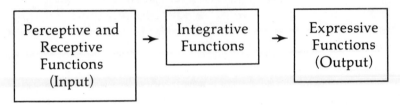

The Receptive Function

Generally, the learning disabled child has difficulty organizing his inner self and the world about him. This difficulty in organization may exist primarily in any one of the three realms. In the receptive function, for example, the learning disabled child may have difficulty in the decoding process, or perhaps, information is perceived but its significance is not understood. Disturbance in this input, or receptive function, can obviously create problems with comprehension abilities. The child simply does not perceive the world in the same way that most of us do.

The Integrative Function

The second area of functioning is the integrative abilities of the child. This process involves the internal manipulation of symbols and includes the ability to relate what is seen and heard to information which has been previously stored. This integrative process involves the formulation of thoughts and provides the link between the environmental input to the individual and from the individual toward the environment. The child confuses and/or cannot remember information which is obtained.

The Expressive Function

The third area of functioning is related to the expressive (output) abilities of the child. The information which has been taken into the child's system and integrated with previous information through consistent symbols usually must be encoded. If the child has great difficulty in expressing ideas in words and gestures, he may well have difficulty in the expressive function. He may be unable to act on his environment in an appropriate manner.

Effect on the Sense Modalities

In addition to the three realms of functioning, the three sense modalities may be affected. The child may exhibit distortions of visual perception, auditory perception, and tactual, kinetic, motor perceptions. *That is, the processes of reception, integration, and expression may be affected in any one of the sensory modalities.* The senses of smell and taste also may be affected but, of course, are less important because they are not so critical to learning or the school adjustment process. Obviously vision, hearing, and touch are vital.

For example, visual-perceptual-motor problems are basic to recognition of letters and numerals and the abilities to write, read, and do arithmetic. Audio-perceptual-motor problems are basic to attention, language production, and responses to the auditory environment. Tactual-perceptual-motor problems are related to learning through physical and feeling sensation.

The concept, then, of *specific* learning disabilities implies that the youngster has a learning problem due to the dysfunction of one or more of the learning functions in one or more of the sense modalities. Psychological tests have been developed to help determine the specific disabilities of each child within each of these sensory areas. Such tests permit a differential diagnosis of the child's specific learning disabilities, and this knowledge facilitates the development of an individual prescription for each child.

The Value of Understanding Technical Processes

Some of you may be saying at this point, "Well that's nice. I understand a little better what a learning disability is. I feel a little smarter. I can impress my friends and family with all of this about intake, integration, and output in the various sense modalities. But really now, so what? I'm frustrated about my child. How can I help him? What does all this have to do with my ability to relate to him? What does this have to do with how he does things at home and in the classroom? And how I do things at home or at school to help him?"

This book is based on the notion that parents and teachers can do a better job of relating to the learning disabled child if they have the knowledge and skills to do so. The questions of what to do and how to do it will be dealt with in subsequent chapters. At this point it is important that you understand your child's problem. Although learning disabilities are complicated, it is still relatively easy to understand the *concept of learning disability*. However, only a learning disabled child can feel what it is like to have these problems. I would like you to participate in the following exercise to help you better empathize with the learning disabled child. Perhaps you can get in touch with some of the feelings the child has and consequently understand him a little better.

A Fantasy Exercise

If I were speaking to you I would ask you to close your eyes, relax, and follow my instructions. As it is, you can read a section of the instructions, sit back, close your eyes, and imagine in your mind's eye the directions which I just provided you.

First, sit back in your seat and relax your body. Close your eyes and notice your body muscles; make them as relaxed as you can. Then, open your eyes and look at the things in front of you.

Notice the details of objects. If there is a light switch, notice where it is. If there are marks on the wall, note where they are. If there is an electrical outlet, observe its position. If anything has writing on it, notice what it says. After getting a clear picture of the details, close your eyes again and, with your eyes closed, imagine the scene you have just observed. In your mind's eye, place the details exactly as they are in reality. Remember where the light switch is; recall where the smudges are, and so on until you have the same scene before you that is actually there. When you have clearly placed the details, open your eyes and read on.

Pretend you are a learning disabled child with a visual perception problem. You have no problems with visual acuity; in fact, your vision is 20/20. You do, however, have difficulty with the reception and perception of visual stimuli. You tend sometimes to perceive input in a different way from most people. But of course, since you are not aware that what you see is not what everyone else sees, you are not conscious of why you are having difficulty. You just know that something is wrong because you are bright enough to know that you are not learning as you should.

After reading this section, please close your eyes and in your mind's eye, move the things on the right over to the left.

Move the things on the left over to the right.

Move down the things which were up; and move up the things which were down.

Still in your mind's eye, move the objects which are close, farther away and move the things which are in the distance, closer.

After doing this, try to tune into your body and notice any tension which has crept in. Try to get in touch with

23

your feelings. When you have done so, open your eyes and read on.

Now pretend you have a reading book in front of you. The book is open and there are interesting pictures at the top of the page and words and sentences at the bottom. The print is fairly large and you can see the page clearly. You begin to read. The first sentence is "It was a dark and stormy night." As you read, the *b*'s look like *d*'s and *d*'s, like *b*'s. The *p*'s look like *q*'s and the *q*'s, like *p*'s. The *n*'s look like *m*'s; the *m*'s, like *n*'s. Close your eyes and imagine the changes.

Still with your eyes closed and still in your mind's eye, you continue to try to read. . . . But words like *was* read like *saw*. Words like *it* seem like *ti*.

And sometimes you start from the right of the page instead of the left.

You are still trying to understand just what the sentence "Ti saw a bark and stormy might" means (or is the sentence "Might, Stormy and dark saw it"?) when the kid next to you finishes his reading assignment, noisily slams his book, and goes out to recess.

You are still trying to understand the sentence when the teacher comes by and says, in a harsh, angry voice, "Would you hurry up. If you would just try harder you would do better at reading." Close your eyes again and imagine the scene. Notice again if any tension has crept into your body. Notice again the feelings you have from the experience. Back into your fantasy. . . .

Then you finish and go out to play, and the kid who sits next to you runs up and says, "Hey, retard! Boy, are you slow!" And you hit him, or cry, or go off to play by yourself, or run away from school.

Hopefully, you were able to get in touch with some of the feelings which a learning disabled child experiences. Keep in mind, of course, that this was for you a fantasy exercise. But every day of his life the learning disabled child exists in a confusing, frustrating, absurd, real world.

He needs our understanding, our acceptance, and our help, and a proper effective learning situation where he can succeed.

3

Systems for Remediation of Learning Disabilities

Introduction

This chapter provides an overview of educational approaches currently used in learning disabilities classrooms. These specialized instructional methods are derived from disparate theoretical orientations. Nevertheless, there are some striking similarities among methods. This creates some confusion at the level of operation because techniques developed in one theoretical position are adopted by individuals operating within an alternate framework. Although this contributes to the confusion that permeates the learning disabilities field, it is useful and in line with the feeling that whatever works is a good method. The various procedures presented in this chapter are grouped according to the following categories: perceptual-motor areas, two test-based approaches, a linguistic and language-based system, a neurological theory, and the multisensory approaches.

Educational Strategies
Perceptual-Motor Areas

Three names most consistently associated with the perceptual-motor approach are Kephart, Barsch, and Getman. Each of these men has made great contributions to the field of learning disabilities. Their ideas, procedures, and training programs are continuing to influence special education.

Newell C. Kephart. In Kephart's text, *The Slow Learner in the Classroom* (1971), he states, "It is logical to assume that all behavior is basically motor, that the prerequisites of any kind of behavior are muscular and motor responses" (p. 79). This statement forms the basis of much of Kephart's theory. Muscular basis of behavior is of prime importance. The first responses of a newborn infant are motor.

A child's very first learnings are motor skills, such as walking. These skills later become motor patterns, such as walking with a goal of getting somewhere. Once individual patterns are learned, they are combined into motor generalizations. Normally, perceptual and motor learning proceed together, giving the child a solid and reliable concept of the world. Kephart relates motor learnings to higher-level skills. He assumes that movement affects perception and perception affects the more complex processes. He further emphasizes the need to develop basic skills in their natural order.

Many children don't have a perceptual-motor world that is stable by the time they begin school. This creates problems for them because they have an inadequate orientation, particularly to time and space.

Kephart's approach stresses the importance of the child's perceptual-motor orientation. This is considered a foundation for conceptual and symbolic development in the classroom. Efficient and consistent motor patterns allow the child to systematize his relationship to his environment. Perceptual data are similarly systematized by being compared with data from the individual's motoric system. The perceptual world of the child and his behavioral world converge through perceptual-motor matching. An organized system of perceptual input and behavioral output allows the child to attack and manipulate symbolic and conceptual material.

Kephart believes that perceptual-motor problems are physical. Children who have not had the appropriate experiences to develop these skills may be disorganized motorically, perceptually, and cognitively when they enter school. The problems have been aggravated by an environment in which children don't need or practice the development of basic abilities, such as eye-hand coordination, temporal-spatial translation, and form perception. The restricted school environment further aggravates the problem, since the child is not given enough opportunity to practice the skills he is lacking.

Remediation is based on the assumption that a child must have a stable spatial and temporal orientation to deal with the symbolic materials presented in school. These orientations can be developed only by projecting learned motor activities into perceptual data and subsequently, correlating the motor and perceptual data. Unless this perceptual-motor match is present, the child is unable to correct any distorted perceptions. If this match is not made, the world is confusing and the child becomes unsure of reality. Many distorted perceptions are like optical illusions. The child doesn't know if he should trust his motor or perceptual cues. An example is the youngster who constantly touches things because he doesn't trust what he sees.

Kephart's training program focuses on the child's sensorimotor learning, his ocular control, and his form perception. Sensorimotor training includes activities requiring the use of large muscles and groups of muscles. Ocular control is developed through remedial techniques for eye control. Corrective tasks requiring matching and reproduction of patterns and forms are necessary for a child with poor form perception.

Ray Barsch. Barsch's theory of "movigenics," that is, the individual's movement in space and the ramification of that movement, provides the basis for much of his work. More precisely defined, *movigenics* is "the study of the origin and development of movement patterns leading to learning efficiency" (Barsch, 1965, p. 5). Therefore, Barsch focuses his approach to learning disabilities on a spatially oriented and movement-in-space program.

Movigenics is based on twelve dimensions (Barsch, 1965) considered important for learning. Barsch (1967) also has detailed specific activities to correspond to these dimensions. The following categories and examples of training activities represent the movigenic curriculum.

Body control and movement through space

> 1. Muscular strength. Heavier exercise, such as jumping rope and lifting.
> 2. Dynamic balance. Walking a balance beam.
> 3. Spatial awareness. Turning upon a direct command (e.g., "turn right; turn left").
> 4. Body awareness. Labeling body parts.

These first four elements apply to control of the body and its movement through space. The child integrates muscular strength with information regarding position, place, and self. He is thus able to move objects and himself according to his needs and environmental demands.

Learning process through senses

> 5. Visual dynamics. Visual tracking, memory, and steering exercise.
> 6. Auditory dynamics. Sound discrimination and imitation activities.
> 7. Kinesthesia. Cutting with scissors and using pegboards.
> 8. Tactual dynamics. Identifying objects by touch.

These four categories (5-8) pertain to the child's learning to process information from visual, auditory, kinesthetic, and tactual modalities. Learning in these areas occurs simultaneously with the child's learning to transport himself through space.

Expansion of performance

9. Bilaterality. Imitating bilateral movements.
10. Rhythm. Developing movement with a rhythmic basis using drums, clapping, and metronomes.
11. Flexibility. Activities possibly including shifting patterns of movement with modification occurring in speed, force, time, and direction.
12. Motor planning. A cognitive rehearsal step which requires knowledge of what is needed and what is available in the movement repertoire.

These last four areas represent "factors which enlarge, enrich, expand, and explicate the performance efficiency of all others" (Barsch, 1965, p. 8).

As can be seen, the orientation of these dimensions and activities is essentially nonlanguage, and the emphasis is upon perceptual-motor learning. Thus, a nonacademically oriented curriculum can be designed to create spatial proficiency.

Gerald N. Getman. As an optometrist, Getman (Getman, 1961; 1962; Getman and Hendrickson, 1966; Getman, et al., 1968) uses the terms vision and perception almost synonymously. He sees vision to be a learned ability to understand things that cannot be touched, tasted, smelled, or heard. Vision refers to the way one understands the world and his relationship to it, and it evolves from the actions of the entire organism. A child thus needs good coordination of body parts to develop perception of symbols and forms.

Getman's (Getman, 1961; 1962; Getman and Hendrickson, 1966; Getman, et al., 1968) theory is based on the idea that each stage of development depends on a lower level and each level is based on certain activities. His model serves as a guideline for mind-body training to help children reach their maximum cognitive development. Beginning at the lowest level, the Getman model is described on the following page.

1. *Innate response system* is unlearned and present at birth. It consists of such things as (a) light reflex (change in pupil size); (b) tonic neck reflex; (c) startle reflex; (d) grasp reflex; (e) reciprocal reflex (thrust-counterthrust of body movements); (f) stato-kinetic reflex (readiness to act); (g) myotatic reflex (stretch).
2. *General motor system* is the system of locomotion and consists of (a) creeping, (b) walking, (c) running, (d) jumping, (e) skipping, and (f) hopping.
3. *Special motor system* provides a combination of skills such as (a) eye-hand, (b) two hands working together, (c) hand-foot, (d) voice, and (e) gesture.
4. *Ocular motor system* pertains to vision and includes (a) fixation (the ability to locate a target); (b) saccadies (movement from one target to another); (c) pursuits (both eyes follow a target); (d) rotation (movement of both eyes in all directions).
5. *Speech motor system* consists of (a) babbling, (b) imitative speech, and (c) original speech.
6. *Visualization system* is the ability to remember what has previously been seen, heard, touched, or felt after the original stimulus has been removed.
7. *Vision/perception system* is learned through earlier developmental skills and is dependent on all of them.

The child progresses through these sequential and interrelated maturational stages. Getman (1962) and Getman and Hendrickson (1966) have provided a collection of training activities which are purported to facilitate learning at each stage. In addition Getman and his associates (1968) have devised six programs of practical lessons for the development of perceptual-motor skills. They are practice in (1) general coordination, (2) balance, (3) eye-hand coordination, (4) eye movements, (5) form recognition, and (6) visual memory.

Two Test-Based Approaches

The Developmental Test of Visual Perception [DTVP (Frostig et al., 1964)] and the Illinois Test of Psycholinguistic Abilities [ITPA (Kirk, McCarthy, and Kirk, 1968)] are currently being utilized in many learning disability programs. Both instruments provide a diagnostic assessment of specific problem and strength areas. Both can lead to individualized curricula designed to remediate the specific problems and utilize the strength areas. Except for the assessment aspect of these theories which make a unique contribution, it would be entirely appropriate to discuss both approaches in other sections of this chapter. The Frostig test and program are oriented to the perceptual-motor system; the ITPA and subsequent program constitute a language-development approach. Because of the emphasis on a scaled, standardized, and formal instrument and because of the remediation procedures emanating from the results of these tests, the approaches are considered here.

Marianne Frostig and the DTVP. Frostig has focused primarily on the area of visual perception. Her orientation stems from Jean Piaget's and Heinz Werner's developmental theories and, in addition, learning theory and psychoanalysis. In 1963 she published her *Developmental Test of Visual Perception,* which evolved from work with children with learning difficulties. Many of these children also appeared to have difficulties in visual perception. The test was designed to provide the basis for exacting remedial techniques, and it specifically differentiates five areas of visual perception skills: (1) eye-motor coordination; (2) figure-ground; (3) constancy of shape; (4) position in space; and (5) spatial relationships.

Frostig's training material (Frostig and Horne, 1964) purports to ameliorate specific disabilities as assessed by the test. Another focus of her material is readiness training, which includes all the necessary abilities normally present upon entering school. While much research (see

32

Balow, 1971) suggests that the transfer from Frostig materials to school-related material is marginal, the Frostig materials are used in many classrooms, providing an important nonspecific addition to the educational curriculum.

Frostig suggests that the child with learning difficulties be evaluated in the following developmental areas: sensory-motor abilities, language, visual and auditory perception, higher-thought processes, social adjustment, and emotional development. The Frostig program calls for four tests prior to beginning remedial instruction. These tests are (1) Marianne Frostig's Developmental Test of Visual Perception, (2) Wepman's (1958) Auditory Discrimination Test, (3) Wechsler Intelligence Scale for Children (1949), and (4) The Illinois Test for Psycholinguistic Abilities. After the child's learning patterns are thus assessed, a curriculum specifically appropriate to the child may be selected, adapted, or developed.

Frostig has developed a four-point plan for remediation (McCarthy and McCarthy, 1969): (1) amelioration of specific developmental lags, primarily through programs focusing on these areas; (2) amelioration of global and pervasive disturbances, such as impulsivity and distractibility, primarily through classroom management techniques; (3) teaching of subject matter and skills; and (4) aiding the child's social adjustment and emotional development.

Samuel A. Kirk and the ITPA. According to Kirk (1966), there is a strong correlation between a child's language ability and his later academic achievement. He assumes that if preschoolers with language difficulties can be differentiated from those with normal language functioning, remediation can and should begin at an early age. This approach may prevent more serious disturbances later when the child is pressured into using more complex linguistic skills. Linguistic ability is defined as the ability to communicate and think in language symbols. Linguistic performance often is affected in children with learning

33

disabilities. To differentiate those children with linguistic difficulties, an instrument must do more than categorize and classify a child. It must point out particular areas of difficulty.

With these factors as a framework, the Illinois Test of Psycholinguistic Abilities was developed in 1961 and revised seven years later (Kirk, McCarthy, and Kirk, 1968). The ITPA diagnoses learning problems by assessing mental functioning in terms of: (a) levels of organization, or the degree to which habits of communication have developed in the child; (b) channels of communication, or the input and output routes through which communication flows; (c) psycholinguistic processes which involve the acquisition and use of language. There are several ITPA subtests designed to sample the above components of mental processes. A lag in any of these areas may underlie a learning disability. The subtests are purported to identify a perceptual, visual, auditory, or kinesthetic malfunction which presumably is the cause of learning disorders. This would indicate that the child does not have appropriate recognition of the world around him. The difficulty often lies with the brain's faulty ability to interpret sense data, although this does not assume that there are neurological correlates of behavior.

Once the child's deficits have been discovered, a staff meeting should be conducted to determine the best remedial steps for that particular child. Since there is rarely a single factor contributing to a learning disability, a multifactor approach should be assumed. The child's assets as well as his liabilities need to be considered. When a deficit is discovered in any area, a series of exercises is prepared to treat that problem. Remedial tasks should be devised to help a child at whatever developmental stage he is.

Several education programs and activity plans designed to remediate problems identified with the ITPA have been developed. Kirk (1966) provides solid direction for remediation in addition to his discussion of diagnosis of learning disabilities. Hartman (1966) developed the Preschool Diagnostic Language Program for educationally disadvantaged children. This program is equally beneficial for children with disorders as well as those who are language deprived. Wiseman (1965) provides a series of language activities separated into five major categories: decoding, association, encoding, closure (automatic) processes, and memory.

Linguistic and Language-Based Systems

Helmer Myklebust. While Kirk combined perceptual-motor and language behaviors in the psychometric approach of the ITPA, the work of Helmer Myklebust (1960) predates and dominates the field in the linguistic area. Myklebust has been prominent in drawing attention to the language problems of learning disabled children.

Myklebust's system classifies children on the basis of whether they have difficulty in processing language inputs, producing language, or a combination of both. The child thus can be identified as having language problems which are primarily receptive, predominately expressive, or mixed. Beyond this system of classification, learning is viewed as a hierarchy of developmental experiences. When one level of development is impaired, each of the areas following that level is presumed to be affected to some degree. The developmental hierarchy detailed by Myklebust (1960) is:

1. *Sensation.* This level refers to nervous system activity which results from data obtained from a given sense organ.
2. *Perception.* The individual interprets sensation and engages in anticipatory behavior.
3. *Imagery.* The actual, physical experience or object is represented by the image or memory and is used in the thought process.
4. *Verbal Symbolic Behavior.* At this level verbal language internalizes experiences, and the individual is able to communicate with others. The verbal includes:

35

the linking of symbols to experience; the comprehension of symbols—receptive language; and the expression of symbols—expressive language.

5. *Conceptualization.* This level includes the categorization and classification of experiences within common elements. Rather than being considered mutually exclusive levels, the individual categories are viewed as developmental, overlapping stages. Failing to master a given level of the hierarchy will result in a corresponding disability which reduces the probability for success at higher levels.

Myklebust and his colleague (Johnson and Myklebust, 1964) have identified five major types of learning disabilities—nonverbal areas, auditory language, reading, writing, and arithmetic. Accurate, differential diagnosis obtained through a comprehensive diagnostic study provides the basis for remediation. Teaching is directed to the type and level of disability with tolerance level and readiness of the child taken into account. The Johnson and Myklebust text, *Learning Disabilities: Educational Principles and Practices* (1964), provides specific training activities and is the best source for remediation procedures based on the model just described.

Other Language Model Systems. Two additional systems that adhere to a language model must be mentioned. The Barry program (1961) includes pertinent and practical information, materials, procedures, and techniques found to be valuable. Her approach seems most suitable for use with younger children. McGinnis (1963) also shares a strong auditory orientation which is reflected in her training program. Her techniques are more appropriate for use with older children and adolescents.

A Neurological Theory

Delacato (1959, 1963, 1966) approaches learning disabilities from a neurologically based point of view. He assumes that in the course of full neurological development, an individual proceeds in an orderly way, anatomically using increasingly higher levels of the central nervous system. If a high level of functioning is incomplete, a lower level becomes operative and dominant. If a lower level is incomplete, all higher levels are affected. If there is an obstruction at any of the lower levels, communication and language dysfunctions occur. Thus, school achievement depends on anatomical development.

The individual's neurological development begins during the first three months of gestation and ends at about six and a half years in normal humans. The neurological development progresses in an orderly fashion vertically through the spinal cord and all other areas of the central nervous system up to the level of the cortex. The developmental progression inside the cortex is lateral— either left to right or right to left. If a lower level is incomplete, all higher levels are affected; similarly if a higher level is not functioning, the lower levels will dominate. The final lateral progression of the cortex, absent in other mammals, must become dominant. If man's organization is to be complete, either his right or left cortical hemisphere must become dominant.

Man has evolved so that there are two hemispheres of the brain which, although they mirror each other, have different functions, i.e., right-handed individuals are one-sided in that they are right-eyed, right-footed, and right-handed with the left cortical hemisphere dominant. Injury or trauma to the dominant hemisphere results in loss of language skills.

Delacato (1966) has identified six symptoms of communication dysfunction in order of decreasing degrees of the same problem: (1) aphasia; (2) delayed speech; (3) stuttering; (4) retarded reading; (5) poor spelling and handwriting; and (6) reading in normal range but problems in mathematical areas. He believes a child treated for one of these problems will show signs of the succeeding problems, i.e., a delayed-speech child is likely also to exhibit stuttering while he progresses through his communication problem. Neurological disorder underlies all of these symptoms and is further enhanced by treatment of these individual symptoms rather than by treatment of the underlying neurological disorganization.

The goal of this theory then is to establish in the brain-injured, retarded, and reading disabled the neurological developmental stages observed in normal children. If the problem lies in the nervous system, that is where the treatment must occur. Underlying Delacato's theory is the assumption that one can succeed in reorganizing the nervous system of a child by revisiting the operations of childhood in a systematic way. Delacato suggests that one can measure the level of neurological organization and can prescribe activities to improve neurological development and learning disorders.

In Delacato's program, treatment typically is initiated at the level of neurological organization indicated in the examination and also is aimed at reorganizing subsequent disorganized levels. Remediation includes exercises at the point of weakness. If the child is unable to make the appropriate movements, they are passively imposed upon him by moving his limbs. Delacato also suggests use of sensory stimulation, breathing exercises, restriction of fluids, and prescribed sleeping positions. Delacato assumes that by repeating or instituting the operations of childhood and working through the various stages of development that occur or should have occurred during childhood, neurological reorganization can take place. Once neurological reorganization has occurred, the learning disability is remediated.

Multisensory Approaches

Grace M. Fernald. Fernald (1943) concentrates her efforts on the remediation of basic school subjects. She suggests a simultaneous stimulation of all input modalities to reinforce learning, with special emphasis on tactile and kinesthetic. Consequently, her system is multisensory because it involves four modalities; i.e., visual, auditory, kinesthetic, and tactile. Referred to as VAKT, the approach is essentially a cognitive one. The words learned always originate with the reader and have meaningful, contextual association.

Fernald noticed that school failures and behavior problems are associated, but she did not assign any cause-effect relationship. She suggested four conditions to cope with this problem.

1. Don't call attention to emotionally loaded situations.
2. Don't use methods by which a person can't learn.
3. Don't cause the child to feel conspicuous or embarrassed.
4. Direct attention to the child's progress.

Fernald's approach suggests a special method for teaching reading and spelling in which the child learns a word as a total pattern. By viewing, writing, saying, and tracing the word, the child strengthens his memory and visualization of the total word.

With this method, a child is told that he is going to learn words in a new way, and he is told to select a word that he wants to learn. The teacher writes the word on a large piece of paper as the child watches, and then the teacher says the word. Next, the child traces the word several times. Following this, he writes it on a separate piece of paper as he says it. The word is then written from memory without looking at the original. If it is incorrect, the tracing and saying steps are repeated. If it is correct, it is placed in a file box. Later, the tracing method is dropped; the child learns a word by looking at it as the teacher writes it and then saying it and writing it himself. Finally he learns the word just by looking at it.

The VAKT is essentially a word-learning technique; the child should have reading instruction individually or in a group to develop comprehension skills. The method presents material in a sequential manner, insures active attention, and reteaches, reinforces, and reviews a word until it is thoroughly learned. By utilizing the child's words and later his stories, the method capitalizes on the child's interest to provide motivation for reading and writing.

William M. Cruickshank. The final theorist to be discussed is Cruickshank (1961). In his attempts at diagnosis, he prefers to keep A.A. Strauss's terminology, "brain-injured child." His rationale is that the inability of the diagnostician to be specific and to obtain positive proof of a brain injury does not imply that no injury to tissue exists. If the diagnostic procedures were available to permit accurate evaluation of children possessing certain characteristic behaviors, tissue damage or injury would most likely be demonstrated and thus the child would accurately be called brain-injured, according to Cruickshank.

Cruickshank proposed that these "brain-injured" children be placed in special classes within the public school system. These classes would contain six to ten children who had been diagnosed as brain-injured, perceptually handicapped, or having minimal brain dysfunction. A wide variety of materials and arrangements would be available to the teacher. Cruickshank's detailed description of special classes has become the prototype for many such self-contained classes.

Often, the school is unable to do much with "brain-injured" children; however, Cruickshank, along with others, has suggested control of the following factors.

1. *Space.* This refers to the physical setting. It should be conducive to learning and might include the use of partitions, cubicles, and screens to rule out any unnecessary distractions. Translucent, rather than transparent, windows are suggested. The teacher's clothing should be simple and free of ornamentation.
2. *Time.* Lessons are to be shortened to accommodate the child with a short attention span.
3. *Multiplicity.* This refers to the number of factors a child must manipulate at once. The child can be given fewer spelling words to complete, fewer

pages to read, and so forth. It may be necessary to limit a lesson to one sense modality at a time.

4. *Difficulty level*. This must be modified to the tolerance level of the child. Learning of skills must follow a natural progression.
5. *Language*. This should be reduced to clear and simple statements appropriate to the child's ability to understand.
6. *Interpersonal relationship factor*. The teacher and student must have good rapport for learning to take place.

The goal of special classes is to help children organize themselves for increased independent learning so that they will eventually be able to return to the normal class. The return to normal classes is usually accomplished through a gradual phasing-in process.

Conclusion

In this chapter a variety of educational approaches has been discussed. Hopefully, the reader will gain some understanding of the procedures which are being used to remediate learning disability problems. The parent who understands the school program and the rationale behind particular techniques can provide more support for that program and for the child. The teacher who understands the wide range of teaching strategies can develop approaches to fit a particular child. The authors within each of the areas provide a variety of strategies, programs, and techniques designed to help the learning disabled child. By understanding the various approaches, the teacher and parent of the handicapped child can truly encourage the learning process.

4

Specific Learning Disabilities: Visual Perception Problems

Introduction

Life and learning go on in a world filled with visual stimuli. Our visual abilities provide us with a major learning channel and constitute one of the most important means through which we receive information about our social and physical world. Some writers have estimated that 80 percent of a child's learning takes place through the eye. Getman (1962) equates vision with intelligence; he states: "vision and intelligence are very closely related. What a child sees and understands he can know—what a child knows determines his cultural intelligence " (p. 20).

Many people believe that the term *vision* is synonymous with the term *seeing*. This is not the case. Ability to read an eye chart and pass the popular Snellen eye test with a 20/20 score is an indication of good visual *acuity*. However, acuity, which is a term to denote visual clarity, is only one aspect of vision. In a more inclusive sense, *vision* can best be described as *meaningful seeing*. Many learning disabled children with good visual acuity fail according to this definition. With a learning disabled child, the difficulty often lies with the inability of the brain to interpret visual data. The primary concern in this discussion is with children who can *see* but who cannot differentiate, remember, or interpret words, probably because of a central nervous system dysfunction.

Problems in visual perception are manifested in the inability of the child to identify, discriminate, remember, and interpret visual sensations. In young children this may be demonstrated in inability to reproduce geometrical forms, figure-ground confusion, object reversals, and rotations. As the child gets older, these problems begin to exhibit themselves in reading letters and words. Needless to say, the youngster with a visual disability suffers severe handicaps in the learning process.

Several areas of specific visual functioning can be involved with a visual learning disability. A number of writers have defined these visual functions. The intent of these writers has been to isolate specific functional problems within the visual modality. Descriptions and definitions of some of these functions follow.

Areas of Visual Functioning
Visual Perception
and Discrimination (Receptive)

Visual perception refers to the ability to comprehend what one sees; i.e., to gain meaning from visual stimuli. A deficit in visual perception is a **visual decoding** or **visual reception disability**; another pertinent term is visual discrimination. Briefly, **visual discrimination** usually refers to the ability to recognize similarities and differences, such as shape, color, and size, among groups of objects. This facility finds its expression in the individual's ability to match letters and numbers. Learning problems in this area arise when the child confuses letters and words that look alike.

Marianne Frostig, a leader in the field, takes a visual perceptual approach to the diagnosis and remediation of learning disabilities. She claims that although the cause of the disability may be unknown, the real issue is that the learning disabled child does not have appropriate recognition of the world around him. She has developed a number of useful tools including the Developmental Test of Visual Perception (Frostig et al., 1964). This instrument is a paper-pencil test which has as its aim the differentiating of various kinds of visual reception and discrimination abilities. Since many of Frostig's concepts fall within the visual reception and discrimination area, they are worthy of comment here.

Object discrimination refers to the ability to recognize differences in shape. The ability to realize the differences between the shape of a square and the shape of a triangle, or between the shape of the letter *e* and the letter *o* is an example. Object discrimination frequently expresses itself in **figure-ground problems**. That is, the child is unable to pay attention to the specific item or figure to which he is supposed to attend but looks instead at all the stimuli in the background. In attempting to read, the child is not able to focus on the specific letter or word.

Form constancy is the ability to recognize a form in spite of nonsignificant variations in shape, position, size, or texture. Closely related to form constancy is the problem of **object constancy**. Each time the learning disabled child with this problem looks at something, he may perceive it differently. Obviously, if forms and objects seem different each time he sees them, it becomes impossible for him to learn their shapes. One task for the child who is visually disabled may be to learn how to see objects in the same way each time he looks at them so that he can learn to recognize them.

Recognition of the rotation of forms in space is the ability to notice the difference between a triangle standing on its base and one standing on its point. Children having this ability are able to distinguish a particular form from

44

other figures as it is presented in an identical, reversed, or rotated position. The mastery of position in space is needed to differentiate letters which have the same form but different positions, such as b and d, p and q.

Another aspect of visual reception, **discrimination problems** involve the perception of space and spatial relationships. These areas concern the ability to perceive the positions of two or more objects in relation to each other and in relation to the observer. Problems in these areas often find their expression in reversals of letters and words. Frequently, the reversals a child sees, such as was for saw, may be due to reading backward. That is, his eyes scan the word from right to left. This occurs as a laterality problem for such children, and they must be taught to scan words from left to right only. On the other hand, some children actually see the words or letters backwards. The laterality and directionality problem will be discussed later in this chapter.

Visual Association (Integration)

To understand the information which a person receives through his visual senses, he must be able to organize, manipulate, categorize, and generalize the visual impressions in a meaningful way. This process occurs at a representational level, requiring complex thinking with symbols. For example, each time an individual sees a cat, he must be able to differentiate it as a species of animal, categorize it as a cat, and subcategorize it as a gray cat. As the child learns to read, he also must extend the concept of the actual physical cat to the various visual configurations denoting cat in the written form: CAT, cat, *cat*, and *cat* ; to the spoken word, "cat"; and to pictures of various cats.

The learning disabled child who has difficulty with visual association and integration may be unable to organize his visual impressions; he may be unable to generalize from his storage of impressions to make the connections between one cat and others, between a kitten and a cat, between the written and the spoken word, or between the animal and the written word. Rather than being faulty at abstract thought, a popular misconception, the learning disabled child often is *faulty at generalizing and categorizing abstract concepts.*

Visual Memory (Integration)

Another area of concern in the visual modality is the function of visual memory. Some writers (Reger, Schroeder, and Uschold, 1968; Bannatyne, 1971) suggest that there are two types of memory problems that are frequently found in learning disabled children. They are (1) immediate memory and (2) accurate recall of prior visual experiences. **Immediate memory** focuses on the child's inability to store symbols. This type of memory problem is observed in the child who can recognize letters, numbers, or words only momentarily. The child with an immediate memory problem usually reads at a preprimer level or is a nonreader. He has difficulty in arithmetic, writing, and spelling.

With a **recall memory problem**, the child can recognize the symbol when given a model, but he cannot remember it by himself. That is, if the child can see a 2, he remembers what it is, but he cannot recall the 2 without a visual cue. In other words, the individual cannot re-visualize symbols. A child with a problem of this nature often can read fairly well, although he may be two or three years below grade level. He most likely will experience great difficulty in writing and spelling.

Johnson and Myklebust (1964) describe a 14-year-old nonreader who could neither describe his home nor remember whether his very blond brother had light or dark hair. They point out that this "revisualization deficit may affect other forms of behavior so that numbers, musical notes, or other types of figures cannot be remembered" (p. 153). Obviously, the greatest problem for the child arises in memory for the printed word.

46

Visual Sequential Memory (Integration)

Another important visual ability is that of visual sequencing. Tasks which require a child to sequence also require him to remember. Consequently, **visual sequential memory** refers to the ability to remember a sequence of visual stimuli. Difficulty may be exhibited in this area by the inability to write from memory a word or letter sequence which is presented visually. Also, a tendency for reversals of letters in reading, spelling, and writing indicates a possible visual sequencing problem.

Specifically, visual sequential memory is necessary for developing a sight vocabulary and for spelling and writing skills. A child with a deficit in this area may misspell his own name and not recognize that it is misspelled. If a child has a deficit in visual sequential memory, it will be evident at the beginning stage of reading. The child will not be able to retain the visual gestalt of words—the total configuration. He also will evidence reading problems during the final *integration* stage. Speed of reading, dependent upon the rapid visual recognition of words, is likely to be slow. Obviously the child cannot develop speed and comprehension if he must sound out each word as if he had not seen it before. This child also will have difficulty in writing and in spelling and may transpose letters. When visually editing his writing, he will not see the errors.

Visual-Motor Skills (Expressive)

Some learning disabled youngsters may be able to perceive and integrate a visual configuration properly but cannot reproduce it on paper. **Visual-motor coordination**, the skill involved here, is the ability to coordinate vision with the movements of the body or part of the body. The skills in the visual-motor area are normally accomplished through visual perception and an integrated motor response. In addition, this particular skill often involves a degree of tactile and kinesthetic perception as well as

47

adequate understanding of spatial relations. Frequently, the child will recognize that he is distorting the shape of his numbers and letters, but he is unable to convey the message to his hands to reproduce the impression accurately. Needless to say, his spelling and writing suffer.

Laterality and Directionality

Laterality and directionality are considered by some authors (Kephart, 1971; Kirshner, 1972) to be the facilities which undergird each of the preceding areas of visual perception abilities. **Laterality** is usually referred to as the internal awareness of the two sides of the body. That is, laterality is the internal awareness within the body in distinguishing left from right. *Laterality is not innate; it is learned through the trial and error sensory and motor experiences of the infant and young child.* By experimenting with the forces of gravity, the infant develops balance and learns to control his body to gain the important knowledge of one side versus the other. This balance and body awareness process continues throughout early childhood.

Directionality is the projection into space of this internal awareness of sides. *Directionality also is not innate but the result of the application of laterality onto the environment.* It involves the labeling or structuring of the world into reasonable coordinates. As the child projects outside himself through directionality, he establishes objective space. He projects the directions from himself to space, of up-down, left-right, and fore-aft.

A child who has not developed laterality and directionality often has difficulty in seeing the difference between m and w in reading or in reproducing b and d in writing. Indeed, many of the symbols in the alphabet depend on direction in their discrimination (e.g., $b, d, p, q, m,$ w, s, z). If laterality and directionality are developed, the child usually does not have difficulty with those letters and numbers that are commonly reversed. The learning disabled child may have to learn to coordinate the left- and right-side nervous systems, since they are by nature semi-independent systems, in order to develop the correct motor directions essential to the reading tasks.

The direct application of laterality and directionality to the development of reading ability is a controversial issue. It seems clear that motor, balance, laterality, and directionality exercises are able to improve many children's ability to perform these skills as well as to improve their muscle control, coordination, and balance. However, the evidence is less clear whether the ability to read is materially improved by these exercises. Attention to these facilities is included here because the exercises are used in many programs for the learning disabled, because they may be found eventually to affect visual perception skills and consequently reading, and because they do seem to improve the child's self-image, self-confidence, and social acceptance.

An Experiential Exercise

Besides having an intellectual understanding of the technical aspects of the problems facing the child who is visually learning disabled, significant adults—parents, teachers, counselors, psychologists—must have an emotional understanding. Hopefully, the following exercise will allow the reader to tune in to her own frustration and anxiety as she attempts to read the following passage. This simulation may make it easier to empathize with the thoughts and feelings of the child who is learning disabled.

As you complete this exercise try to stay with the experience as long as you can. You can understand the meaning if you try hard enough, so it is important to spend enough time on the exercise to experience the frustration inherent in the task. Pretend that you are a third- or fourth-grade learning disabled child with visual perception, visual discrimination, and laterality problems. Be sure to answer the four questions at the end of the exercise before you read the translation. Pretend also that you will be graded on your performance on these questions. Your self-confidence, self-esteem, and social approval hinge on how well you do. Also, the adults who are important to you have absolutely no understanding and/or appreciation of your problem. Consequently, the teacher is likely to say as you are trying to finish this exercise and in rather harsh tones, "Hurry up; you don't try hard enough; if you would stop fooling around you would do better work."

Gobbledygook

hTe cbilb wi tha learn ingdis adility wust frepuemtly ex geri enceana n alicein won berl an beffect Hemust coge wi thhaph azarb perc eptions anuns table wor ldaub in consisten tadults. Freq
u

e

n

t

lyhe is frust rated dyh is rep eated fail ures pres sureb dy hte lengthof ti me he hasto boh is worka nb confused by hte crasy zift mg zymdolswe give him.Be cause hedoe snotl earm inhte tradi tion alway, me wust t each hin dif fer ently.I wo uldlike totelly oum ore adout hin.

1. hTe le arnind is able dchild isac hilb of ave rage or adove ave rage in tell igence.
2. ob vi ousbe fectso fhte cen tralner vous yz ten nay degresent or adsent; hte ch ilb,ho

w

e

v

e r,probably benomztr ates dis abilit ities inper ception co n cep tion,int egra tionan dacad emic achi eve mentei thre zeber ate lyorin condimat ion.htese bist urb amces aren ot dueq ri marily tas em sor yloss, memtalr et arb ation,enotionol bis tnrb amce, o rem vironmnemt albis abvam tage. thiA ought ea chch ildis amin bivdual, ther eare sone q eneral char acter istics. htese lw ill list an dyou c anol ok then up.

3. So me ofteh nor epre va lemts ymtoms seen tobe:
   a. Pro blemz ofV isual Perc ebtiom
   d. Pro blemz of Au dit oryPer ctiom
   c. P

      r

        oblemsofMo tor Ac tiyitv
   b. Pro blemz ofEm onti ality
   e. P roble msof Attenion
   f. Prob lem sof Con ception
   g. yromeM ofsnelborP.

teLus won dis cus ssom easp cetz ofy our vis ual perc epti npor blens.

1. Wh atmere zone ofyour re actions—tou hghtsan btee lings—wh ile yon at tenp tedtor eadth is?
2. tiLs som eof hte hting htat ma dey ourr eading- taslc nor edif Fuiclt.
3. tiLs som eof hte htings yondid tbaten abled yo utor eadthis ecercise.
4. Lis tan yi deasy duhave htat canb en sed toh elpother adn itz toebx erieuce bercebtnal broplens.

After struggling with the above exercise, read the following passage to see if you were able to understand the "foreign language" which perceptual problems of a visual nature create for learning disabled children.

Gobbledygook

The child with a learning disability must frequently experience an "Alice in Wonderland" effect. He must cope with haphazard perceptions, an unstable world, and inconsistent adults. Frequently he is frustrated by his repeated failures, pressured by the length of time he has to do his work and confused by the crazy, shifting symbols we give him. Because he does not learn in the traditional way, we must teach him differently. I would like to tell you more about him.

1. The learning disabled child is a child of average or above-average intelligence.
2. Obvious defects of the central nervous system may be present or absent; the child, however, probably demonstrates disabilities in perception, conception, integration, and academic achievement either separately or in combination. These disturbances are not due primarily to sensory loss, mental retardation, emotional disturbance, or environmental disadvantage. Although each child is an individual, there are some general characteristics. These I will list and you can look them up.
3. Some of the more prevalent symptoms seem to be:
    a. Problems of Visual Perception
    b. Problems of Auditory Perception
    c. Problems of Motor Activity
    d. Problems of Emotionality
    e. Problems of Attention
    f. Problems of Conception
    g. Problems of Memory

Let us now discuss some aspects of your *visual perception problems.*

1. What were some of your reactions—thoughts and feelings—while you attempted to read this?
2. List some of the things that made your reading task more difficult.
3. List some of the things you did that enabled you to read this exercise.
4. List any ideas you have that can be used to help other adults to experience perceptual problems.

If you were able to get in touch with your feelings during this exercise, then perhaps you better understand the frustrations the learning disabled child faces. Remember that for you the frustration ended with the translation; for the learning disabled child, it continues.

Conclusion

Children who experience visual problems have serious learning handicaps. The handicaps are made more serious precisely because they are invisible to significant adults. Consequently, parents, adults, and others concerned with children must begin to recognize the problems and issues involved in visual handicaps. This chapter has focused upon the need to understand and recognize the problem. In addition to understanding and recognizing the problem, adults need to have procedures which might be helpful to the child. The next chapter is designed to provide some of these procedures.

5

Activities for Visual Problems

Introduction

This chapter is devoted to specific activities, tasks, procedures, and games which teachers and parents can utilize to help the learning disabled child with visual handicaps. The strategies described probably need to be refined, changed, and augmented by the reader to suit the specific needs of each unique child in each unique setting.

Teachers and particularly parents need to be aware that the use of the activities poses some potential hazards. For one thing, the maximum benefit of any activity is to focus on the specific learning dysfunction and build the activity to help remediate that problem. Consequently, a parent can maximize his effects by coordinating his efforts at home under the direction of the learning disability specialist. That is, if the teacher, counselor, or psychologist can pinpoint the child's difficulty and suggest specific tasks, the parent's efforts can be most beneficial. The same situation is true in the classroom. The teacher needs to become aware of the specifics of the learning deficits.

These activities are designed to supplement an educational program. If they *become* the program, they are hazardous in the sense that the child misses the benefits of a more definite program.

Another possible problem in making use of this section is the negative feelings which may be engendered in the adult while she works with the child in these activities. Recognize that you are approaching the child in areas where he has a handicap; set your expectation level accordingly. Recognize that the development and integration of the basic skills involved here require a long time to internalize. Recognize that *you* may become frustrated, annoyed, and guilty. If this happens, stop the activity. Work on getting *your* feelings congruent before starting again. By all means, don't transfer your frustration and anxiety to the child; he is carrying enough of his own frustration and anxiety already.

An underlying principle of which parents, in particular, must be cognizant is *DO NOT PRESSURE THE CHILD*. Approach these exercises as a fun thing to do. When the child gets tired or shows disinterest, stop the activity and return to it later. To make the learning disability less traumatic, recognize the child's frustration and provide firm, warm guidance. When the task involves helping with home or school chores, be aware that you are giving him an activity that is most difficult for him to accomplish. Require him to finish it but be careful of overly frustrating him. Also, be careful of emphasizing the competitive aspects of the games which are mentioned, especially with the learning disabled's siblings. There is no benefit in accenting the learning disabled child's low self-esteem.

Tasks for Visual Perception and Discrimination (Receptive)

• Urge the learning disabled child to notice the similarities between colors in pictures and those same colors in nature. Later give the child a piece of paper with a block of color in one corner. Direct him to search through old magazines and cut and paste any object which is the same as the target color.

• Call attention to the property of circles, squares, and other geometrical objects. For example, use the outlines of highway signs for shape discrimination.

• Request that the child notice the figure in a background. Bookstores frequently carry workbooks which have shapes and forms hidden within pictures. These are most useful in helping the child in discerning figure-from-ground images.

• Utilize dot-to-dot pictures with both numbers and letters forming animals and familiar objects.

• Give the learning disabled child the task of separating spoons, forks, and knives into the silverware tray.

• Have him separate tools, buttons, nuts, bolts, nails, and screws.

• Encourage the child to separate triangles, circles, squares, and rectangles as well as sticks of varying size and color. Frequent practice in sorting objects is a useful process.

• "Stick-O-Mats" and "Color-Shapes" by the Judy Company are useful for developing perception of size, shape, and color.

• "Scan" by Parker Brothers is also an excellent game for developing visual constancy.

• Have the child construct models in three dimensions.

• Encourage the child to build simple designs with blocks, parquetry blocks, beads, and peg boards. This is helpful in developing understanding of spatial relations.

• Ask the child to pick out a designated letter from a container of (dry) alphabet cereal. When he locates it, he is allowed to eat it. As he becomes more skilled, increase the number required (e.g., "Find four B's now") and ask him to assemble simple words (e.g., "Spell *dog*").

• Use card games such as "Old Maid," "Go Fish," and "Slap Jack." These and other matching games provide useful practice in visual discrimination. Use similar rules but make use of cards with shapes, letters, or words.

• Use Scrabble letters, cutout letters, and anagrams to show changes in words with the substitution of single letters (e.g., *tip* to *top* to *tap* with the change of *i* to *o* to *a*).

Tasks for Visual Association (Integration)

• Have the child close his eyes and describe what he has seen. Such activities help him develop the ability to visualize or picture what is there.

• When the child sees a dog, have him discuss similarities and differences between that particular dog and other dogs, between dogs and other animals.

• Point out to the child differences and likenesses in letter shapes, in word shapes.

• Present pictures or objects of which all but one are members of a category or set. Ask the child to indicate the nonmembers and explain how they are different.

• Cut apart comic strips and have the child place the squares in their proper sequence. A variation is to have the learning disabled child and his friends and siblings cut apart the strips and then exchange them. Have the children describe the situation and story. Prior to reading development, have the child guess the story with only a few clues.

• Have the child develop a scrapbook from old magazines. Encourage him to think about themes or common elements to put in his scrapbook.

• Have the child cut pictures (later words) from old magazines and group them into various categories and classifications. Emphasize relationship connections by having the child match various occupations with uniforms, equipment, and functions.

• Utilize family photographs to have the child relive or recall experiences.

• Play "Twenty Questions." Present a photograph of a recent vacation and say, "I am thinking of _____."

• Play games based on categories of particular things, such as animals, fruit, vegetables, and so forth. For example, say, "A dog is an animal. Pick four other animals." The difficulty can be increased by requesting that the selection be limited to animals smaller than a dog or perhaps animals that live on the farm.

Tasks for Visual Memory and Sequencing (Integration)

• Place several objects before the child who examines them for color, content, order, or position. When he closes his eyes, the objects can be rearranged, inverted, or removed. With the use of his visual sense, the child can rearrange the objects into their color, order, position, or content.

• A variation of the above activity is to have the child view as many as 10 or 12 pictures or objects for a very short time. Hide or cover the objects and have the child name as many as he can. Later this can be done with letters and words.

• Using a peg board, have two or more youngsters in turn make a design, allow the other(s) to see it while the first child counts to 10. See who can reproduce it from memory.

• Encourage the child to play memory games with himself; for example, remembering what he had for dinner last night, telling the plot of a recent television program or movie, and memorizing license plate numbers on the way to and from school.

• Using the previously mentioned alphabet cereal, ask the child to remember one or more letters; if the child can remember and find the appropriate letters, he may eat them.

• Have the child play "Concentration" card game. An ordinary deck of cards is distributed face down on the table. The person who is first turns over a card, showing its face to the other players. He then attempts to match it by turning over another card. If he makes a match, he keeps both cards and continues; otherwise, both cards are replaced face down on the table. The one with the most cards at the end of the game wins.

• Use variation of the preceding game, having an individual play by himself against time. The same game can be played with letter and word cards as well.

• Play the "What's This" game. Have the child determine what the correct word is when presented with scrambled letters [e.g., a t c (cat), h t e (the), o y b (boy)].

• Have the child make visual maps from memory of different routes to and from school or the market. Ask him to define the number of blocks and the number of houses along the way. Ask him to color certain obvious landmarks (e.g., color the big pink house).

Tasks for Visual-Motor Activity (Expressive)

• Use activities which require drawing, coloring, painting, pasting, and cutting. They are useful processes for visual-motor skills. Use media other than just paper and pencil. Patience and encouragement from the adult are essential to develop a positive attitude for these activities.

• Use activities such as dropping marbles or coins into a can, winding yarn on a spool, pinning clothespins on a line, or dealing cards. They are useful for visual-motor skill. Be alert for other hand and finger exercises.

• Use commercial or self-made mazes. A variation is to have the child himself and his siblings or classmates make simple mazes and share them.

• Have the child stack blocks as high as possible before they topple down. An interesting variation is to make houses of cards.

• Use commercial sewing cards that provide pictured objects which the child can outline by sewing through the card with thread or yarn.

59

- Play, "Chase the Light," which requires two flash-lights and a darkened room. One child points the beam at a wall, floor, or ceiling; the second child tries to follow or "catch" the light with his beam.
- Encourage the many children's games which involve visual-motor integration: ball and jacks, marbles, hop-scotch, jump rope, dodgeball, wooden paddles with a rubber ball attached by a rubber band, and many others.
- Encourage tossing and catching activities with a ball, beanbag, wadded paper, all of which are very effective. If the child has difficulty with these objects, use a balloon until he gains more skill and confidence.

Tasks for
Laterality and Directionality

- In all of the child's activities, the adult should be alert for left-to-right progression and should attempt to bring into consciousness the child's need to distinguish left from right. When reading to the child, when looking at pictures, and when playing games, point out the left-right progression.
- When helping the child with his coat, rather than saying, "Put your arm through," say, "Put your *right* arm through."
- A ring for the child's hand is a good cue for him. It should be on the left or right hand, depending on whether the child is left- or right-handed.
- Since balance is the primary method of developing laterality, the adult should seek to place the child in every conceivable mobile and stationary position that demands balance: standing, sitting, kneeling, lying, etc.
- Balance-beam activities are most useful for laterality training. A two-by-four placed on its edge, a thick rope, or even a strip of masking tape in a line on the floor can serve as a "cliff" for the child to walk along without falling off. Chaney and Kephart (1968) have developed a comprehensive list of balance-beam exercises including walking

the beam frontward, backward, and sideways.

- "T" stools and balancing boards are useful. A "T" stool is a seat with only one leg supporting it. A balance board can allow for incorporating balance in two directions and then in four. Allow the child to balance in sitting, kneeling, and standing positions.
- Utilize innertubes (tractor-size), barrels, and beach balls to help develop balance.
- Plan your trips across town with a street map. Have the child start with his home address and then direct him to the desired destination (e.g., "With your finger go one block west, turn right, go one block and turn east and go six blocks"). Have him take the map and follow the route.

Tracing and other tactile activities may prove to be helpful practices. For example, the "screen technique" is useful. Put a piece of black paper over a small window screen. Write a letter (or number, word, or shape) on the paper with crayon. Have the child trace the image with his finger.

Conclusion

The tasks presented in this chapter are calculated to improve the child's visual skills. There tends to be a high intercorrelation between many of the visual skills—spatial awareness, figure-ground, and visual motor, for example. Consequently, many of the activities or their modifications are mutually facilitating in other areas. The preceding tasks are intended to serve as guides for the imaginative adult to develop further activities for visual-perception training. Thus the interested teachers or parents are highly encouraged to extend these suggestions into ideas and activities of their own devising.

In addition to actually improving visual perception, tasks presented here should provide personal recognition of success and accompanying positive attention from significant adults. Perhaps even more important than gains in the visual area are the quiet moments spent in close, supportive contact.

6

Specific Learning Disabilities: Auditory Perception Problems

Introduction

If the visual channel is the most important learning pathway, then the auditorial channel must run a very close second. For one thing, hearing is the primary channel for interpersonal communication and for language acquisition. Hearing also is the individual's primary scanning sense, i.e., the basic avenue through which one maintains contact with the environment. In fact, many writers consider the audio-perceptual process even more crucial to learning than the visual process. Some programs (Johnson and Myklebust, 1964; McGinnis, 1963) attribute reading disability primarily to auditory deficits and focus on them.

Difficulties Limiting Research

Given the importance of hearing, it may seem odd that there is less information about this function as it relates to learning disabilities than there is about some other functions. A survey of the field of perception reveals considerable theoretical and empirical material on the topic of visual perception. The topic of hearing lags behind, and our understanding of auditory perception is relatively limited. Most of the information we have is based on theoretical neurological explanations rather than applied research.

Much of the difficulty is due to the technical problems associated with research in the auditory area. For example, one major drawback to research in auditory perception has been the difficulty with instrumentation for the production of controlled sound stimuli. For the past hundred years researchers interested in hearing have used a variety of instruments—bells, whistles, noisemakers, tuning forks —to produce sounds to elicit responses in infants and children. Because these instruments have produced such variable differences in tone, timbre, and loudness, experimenters have found it difficult to compare the results of their work.

Another area of difficulty has been in determining a reliable and meaningful response. Here again, a variety of responses, including heart and respiration rates, eyeblink and movement, conditioned sucking and foot withdrawal, have been used to determine the presence of auditory sensitivity in infants and young children. With older children many of these same responses plus verbal and pointing responses, button pushing, and EEG have been used. Results of many studies have been equivocal because of differences in adaption and attention factors. Problems are inherent because of the fact that a total lack of response to an auditory cue cannot be considered as empirical evidence for a child's inability to hear.

The final, and perhaps most important, reason for limited research with learning disabilities of an auditory nature is due to the problems facing the deaf and severely hard-of-hearing child. This fact has tended to attract the efforts of researchers, who most often have focused on the improvement of communication skills and upon the development of techniques for the detection of auditory handicaps. Consequently, there has been relatively little information on the development of auditory processes and auditory skills in youngsters with less dramatic problems.

Stages in Development of Auditory Abilities

Investigations of auditory disabilities have yielded limited information. However, we have been able to identify successive stages in the development of auditory abilities (Lewis, 1951; Hardy, 1956; Penfield and Roberts, 1959). First, a child learns to identify and recognize sounds in his environment; he then makes finer distinctions between various sounds and begins to remember those familiar sounds. Finally, he develops the ability to speak.

Typically, the developmental stages of response to sound are in accord with the following pattern of maturation. The newborn responds to loud noises by becoming startled or crying. After two weeks, the infant demonstrates a listening attitude to the sound of a human voice. By four weeks he is quieted by sound, and his activity is reduced by an approaching sound. By eight weeks he no longer appears disturbed by loud noises, but he accepts these as part of his environment; during this period there also is acute attention to the human voice. By four months there is deliberate head turning in search of voice or sounds. Prior to the sixth month the baby can correctly localize a bell rung on either side of him, and he can discriminate between angry and friendly conversation. In the eighth and ninth month a child attempts to imitate sounds. Further, he is able to respond to his name and simple commands such as "no-no." This suggests the rudiments of language comprehension by the child. These early sounds are differentially reinforced; those sounds which receive attention stay a part of his repertoire.

Much of the child's time is spent in learning how to listen during the first year of life. Listening is a learned ability, whereas the ability to hear is innate (although, of course, hearing is dependent on an intact and functioning auditory mechanism). After this stage, the child is preparing to speak. As the hearing of the child is stimulated by his daily experiences and as his attention span increases, the child learns to decode and encode messages. At two years he has developed "demonstrable speech," which is the use of verbal symbols in relation to direct communication. The major steps in linguistic learning have occurred during the first two years of life. Some researchers (Chomsky, 1957; Lenneberg, 1964) suggest that after age two the child adopts the syntax, phonology, and semantics of his language by abstracting the rules necessary to generate all the sentences of the language. From this point on, the individual consistently connects his life experiences with his symbol-making and symbol-using abilities.

Disabilities in Areas of Auditory Functioning

A child with an auditory learning disability is inhibited in learning through the auditory channel. The child hears but does not interpret what he hears. As in the visual modality, the problem is not with acuity (**auditory acuity** is sharpness or acuteness of hearing). The child does hear sounds and in tests which measure acuity does not demonstrate any abnormalities. However, the youngster may be unable to structure his auditory world—to sort out sounds and associate them with particular experiences or objects. A child who is severely handicapped in these fundamental aspects of auditory perception often is mistakenly considered hard-of-hearing or deaf.

As in visual functioning, problems in auditory processing have been divided into several separate but interlinking functions. Briefly these functions are: (1) auditory perception and discrimination—hearing similarities and differences between sounds, (2) auditory memory—the immediate and delayed recall of information obtained by

65

ear, (3) auditory sequencing—the recall of sounds which fall in a particular order, (4) auditory-vocal association and comprehension of auditory information—the integration of auditory data, and (5) auditory expressive language. These areas are considered in a more detailed fashion in the following sections.

Auditory Perception and Discrimination (Receptive)

Auditory perception and discrimination are the abilities to understand what is heard, to gain meaning from auditory stimulation. Some authors refer to a deficit in auditory reception as an auditory decoding disability, and others refer to it as auditory receptive problems. This confusion probably is due to the two-phase process which is involved in auditory perception. *First a child has to receive auditory stimuli and then he must associate the auditory stimuli with its referent.*

A child with a specific disorder in this area is unable to relate the appropriate unit of experience to the spoken word. The child hears but does not understand. In less severe cases, there is understanding of some words, but not of others. For example, the child may comprehend simple nouns, but not words that represent action, qualities, feelings, or ideas. Children with auditory perception and discrimination disabilities often have poor auditory memory and are deficient in other auditory abilities, such as rhyming, sound blending, or identifying sounds. They frequently request information to be repeated. They show confusion when given directions or commands. The child may be unable to respond to a verbal command but yet can respond to a gesture or nonverbal command. Some children are unable to attend to a particular sound unless they hear it in total silence. Other sounds interfere with their zeroing in on auditory stimulus. They cannot isolate one sound from background sounds, thus demonstrating an auditory figure-ground problem.

Problems frequently arise with the misperception of some of the sounds the child hears because he confuses them with sounds that have similar distinctive features. Jakobson (1968) has categorized letter sounds, blends, and phonemes into their distinctive features. The interested reader may wish to pursue this further. Some common confusions are *p* and *b*, *c* or *e* for *g*, and *ch* and *sh*. The child may also have problems in enunciating precisely because he has not heard the sound appropriately. This problem extends to words, so the child may go to get his *cup* instead of *cap* or a *coke* instead of *coat*. Such a child usually becomes quite skilled at guessing from the context of the message the words he misperceives. Needless to say, spelling dictation highlights his auditory confusion, and he may be a horrible speller.

Auditory Memory (Integration)

Not only must sounds be identified and discriminated from each other, they also must be stored and available for retrieval. Severe auditory disorders often involve problems of memory and recall. Because every facet of the language process is dependent to some extent on memory, these problems make learning language very difficult; even when language is learned, it may not be firmly established. Many children with learning disabilities have no difficulty in understanding or remembering single words but are limited in the amount of information they can remember at any one time. Consequently, they have difficulty comprehending complex oral instructions or remembering a series of commands.

Short- and Long-Term Auditory Memory. As with visual memory, it is possible to distinguish between short- and long-term auditory memory. If the material to be processed requires two minutes or less, **short-term memory** is involved. Anything requiring over two minutes involves long-term memory. Problems in short-term memory would be evident in children who have trouble repeating an auditory pattern after it has been presented. If these problems are severe, the acquisition of language itself is impaired. *That* *is, information needs to be processed while in short-term memory in order to transfer to long-term memory.* If the child cannot remember a sound within one minute, he is not going to recall it after five or ten minutes. **Long-term memory** refers to the ability of the child to respond to auditory stimuli when there is a delay between the message presentation and the child's response. A child with this problem when asked at the dinner table to take out the garbage after dinner may very well forget to do the chore because he is deficient in this ability.

Factors Related to Memory. Vergason (1968) has suggested that memory is related to such factors as (1) meaningfulness of new material to the child, (2) attention of the child to the stimulus to be remembered, (3) extra practice or overlearning which is practice beyond one errorless trial, (4) recognition by the child of differences and similarities of new material to that which is already learned, and (5) degree of interference when the child is trying to learn. Although Vergason is focusing primarily on memory as it relates to educational learning and his factors are most relevant to teachers, his suggestions have general implications for parents. If a child has been evaluated as having auditory memory problems, finding ways to increase one or more of the preceding five points will aid in improving his memory. Some concrete suggestions for doing this are included in the following chapter which focuses on activities for auditory problems.

Auditory Sequential Memory (Integration)

Another auditory function which is related to memory facility is sequential memory. Children with a learning disability in this area may have difficulty understanding or remembering what they hear in a temporal sequence or in a sequence pattern. Characteristically, if given several commands in sequence, such as "Close the door, hang up your coat, and take out the trash," they may rush off and perform the first task but simply not remember the others. Children with this auditory problem tend to do poorly on

68

digit-span tests, such as those found on the Wechsler Intelligence Scale for Children (1949) and the Stanford-Binet intelligence tests (Terman and Merrill, 1960). They also have difficulty on tests of rote memory of a series of nonsense syllables. Further, parents and teachers of children with deficits in auditory memory often express frustration with the children's inability to remember vocal instructions.

While **auditory sequential memory** refers to an ability to remember auditory stimuli in the sequence in which they were heard, there are *two major components* to the facility. They are (a) the short-term/long-term memory dichotomy and (b) memory for meaningful and nonmeaningful material. The child's inability to learn his telephone number and street address at a reasonable age and his inability to learn poems, jingles, and prayers are examples of the way in which children are affected with this difficulty.

Auditory-Vocal Association and Comprehension of Auditory Information (Integration)

Auditory-vocal association ability of the individual primarily is the facility to organize and manipulate linguistic symbols in a functional way and implies the ability to think. Disorders which can be subsumed under this category include *auditory processing problems*. These are difficulties with the ability to comprehend spoken language, to categorize it, and to produce the appropriate response. The child who has a deficit in understanding auditory information may have no difficulty in receiving what he hears; he may also have no difficulty in expressing himself. The child's disability is precisely in the area of analyzing and synthesizing information obtained through the auditory channel. Since this ability includes classifying, categorizing, and recategorizing information to form new concepts, needless to say, the child may experience problems in recognizing information in a meaningful way.

Frequently, the child who has the difficulty of auditory comprehension will understand the first few words of a command or message and then become lost in the barrage of sounds. He can respond appropriately when told to put on his shirt. But he may become utterly confused when mother says, "Put on your blue shirt with your brown pants and take your dark blue sweater." The messages may defy the child's ability to classify, organize, and recategorize. Thus, the child does not comprehend.

Auditory Expressive Language (Expressive)

Some learning disabled children with language disorders have no problem in perceiving and understanding spoken words but are deficient in using them to express themselves. Myklebust (Johnson and Myklebust, 1964), a leader in the field of auditory problems of children, delineates three types of problems which differentiate expressive language difficulties. The three common forms are: (1) reauditorization, (2) auditory-motor integration, and (3) syntax and formulation.

Reauditorization problems are characterized by difficulty in recalling words. Children with this learning disability can understand and recognize words; they have stored words, but they cannot retrieve them. In short, the child cannot remember the word for spontaneous usage and consequently experiences great frustration in trying to communicate. The child tries to relate events but often gives up because he simply cannot remember how to express what he wants to say. Frequently, these children resort to pantomime and gesture to communicate their messages.

Auditory-motor integration refers to the ability of the child to say words. The child can understand and remember the word, but he has difficulty associating the word with the auditory-motor patterns required for speaking; he is unable to imitate words. Although the power of movement is intact, the child demonstrates an inability to move the appropriate muscles in a purposeful manner. Wepman and Jones (1961) suggest that problems of this nature are relatively independent of the symbolic process and that the child "understands what is said to him, formulates symbols, has available the syntax of language, but cannot recall or control the motor act of articulation" (p. 81).

Other children experience problems in formulating sentences. They hear and comprehend but speak in single words or short phrases and demonstrate difficulty with **organization** and **syntax**. Children with this problem are prone to distort the order of words or omit words entirely. They tend to make grammatical errors such as incorrect verb tense usage long after such errors have been recognized and corrected by the normal child.

The development of syntax and the corresponding ability to formulate sentences are complex skills which require considerable integration of cognitive processes. A child must be able to understand language, to manipulate symbols, to remember word sequences, and to generalize principles for sentence structure. The child holds in his mind certain structural language patterns and makes inferences about the relationships of words. He then must produce sentences of his own. The child who is unable to do this demonstrates inadequate and incomplete usage of language and subsequent problems in social and academic achievement.

An Experiential Exercise

Although auditory exercises are difficult to recreate without appropriate electronic equipment, the following exercise is provided as a simulation of at least some of the problems of auditorially impaired children. Again, the purpose of the exercise is to provide an emotional understanding of the frustration experienced by the learning disabled child.

The exercise must be continued long enough to assess the subsequent feelings. Continue the exercise until you experience frustration and terminate it when you are aware of this frustration.

To begin, turn on the television, the radio, and the record player simultaneously. Focus your attention on each one separately. Notice how the focus diminishes on the additional stimuli as you direct your attention to one set of sounds. Now try to tune into the normal sounds of the environment.

Notice how the competing stimuli make your communication difficult when you carry on conversation with another person.

Notice the tension creeping into your muscles.

Imagine the frustration which you would experience if your auditory world were this confusing all the time.

Conclusion

This chapter has attempted to describe various problems associated with specific learning disabilities of an auditory nature. A child who demonstrates all of these auditory problems would indeed be disabled. A number of research studies have demonstrated that few children experience problems in all these areas and that in almost all cases the problems are present in only a slight degree or they can be remediated. Consequently, if the child is receiving appropriate work and training in his school setting and if his parents are providing firm encouragement and a nourishing environment, the child should be able to overcome his handicap.

The tasks described in the following chapter are designed to be used at home and/or at school. They are calculated to improve the deficits in auditory functioning.

7

Activities for Auditory Problems

Introduction

The following activities are suggested to supplement the remedial program of children with auditory learning disabilities. As with visual activities, these tasks are suggestive only and need to be augmented by the reader as seems appropriate.

Here again, it is important *not to overpressure* the child. You are attempting to approach the child in an area which has created problems for him; recognize that fact and proceed accordingly. Make the exercise an enjoyable experience for the child. When he becomes fatigued, stop the activity and continue at a later time. Respond to his frustrations with kind but firm understanding.

Tasks for Auditory Perception and Discrimination (Receptive)

• Any activities which help the child recognize gross sounds may be useful. For example, present the child with

73

a set of noisemakers—a toy horn, a bell, drumsticks, and clankers. Stand behind the child and produce sounds or a series of sounds. The child is to reproduce the same sounds from his objects or to reproduce a particular sound.

• Activities which require a response to a sound (or the absence of a sound) may be very useful in developing auditory attention skills. Games, such as "Musical Chairs," "Fruit Basket Upset," "Simon Says," and "Mother May I?" in which children are required to attend to auditory stimuli are good examples.

• Play "Secret Word" game. The adult identifies a "secret word" that the child is to listen for. The adult then reads a story that contains the word. Each time the child hears the word he responds in some fashion.

• Have the child and his siblings, classmates, or friends play a game in which one child tells a story. The others listen and tell the main idea or paraphrase the story.

• Localization of sound can be learned by games which require the child to respond to sounds from his right to left.

• Require him while blindfolded to walk around following the sound of a horn blown by an adult or other child.

• Have the child play rhyming games (e.g., think of all the words that rhyme with *top, Bob, Mom*).

• Have the child name all the words that start with a *different* sound but rhyme with the word you provide (e.g., the adults says, *ill*; the child says *pill, Bill,* and *hill*).

• Present children's rhyming stories such as "Mary, Mary, Quite Contrary" and "Little Jack Horner." The child identifies the words which rhyme.

• Do exercises from *Peabody Language Development Kits*, (Dunn et al., 1965), and use the *Echorder* and the accompanying *A Manual of Speech and Language Training Methods Using the Echorder* (Sommers and Brady, 1964). "Speecho" from Palfrey's School Supply and "Phonetic Quiznio" from J.L. Hammett are also useful.

• Use Action records such as "Dance-a-Story" from

Educational Records Sales to help children to connect visual clues with sounds and teach them to carry out directions.

• Play charades to facilitate the connection of visual clues with sounds.

• When driving in a noise area, have the child listen with his eyes closed and report all the sounds he can discriminate.

• Play "Packing My Bag" game. Ask the child to identify as many things as he can which begin with the same sound as the place he is going to visit. For example, "I am going to Oregon and I will take an *oar*. I will take an *Oreo*."

• Help the child by using short, one-concept phrases.

• Ask short questions.

• Use visual aids—written material, gestures and so forth—to help the child understand what he hears.

Tasks for Auditory Memory (Integration)

Parents and teachers could improve their relationships with children with both auditory memory and auditory sequential memory problems by simply giving one command at a time. Frequently, adults give the child a series of commands such as, "Hang up your coat, shut the door, and take out the trash." A better procedure with memory-deficient youngsters is to break up the commands into small units and follow through on the completion of the task. (For example, say, "Hang up your coat." See that the child does it. "Shut the door." See that he does it. "Take out the trash." See that he does it.) Be sure always that the child is looking directly at you when you give him instructions. You must have his attention.

• Require that the child imitate a pattern of handclaps or taps on glass, box, can, or drum. Variation can be provided by modifying the tempo, rhythm, and accent. Sequential memory can be strengthened by requiring the correct order of sounds.

• Tell a short story of a few sentences and have the child

retell it. Ask him to repeat it several hours later.
- When making a casserole or salad, recite the ingredients to be put in. Deliberately leave out something and request the child to identify it. Begin with a small list and gradually increase both the list and the omitted items.
- Read a sentence and ask the child to repeat it verbatim. Reread the sentence and leave out a word which the child then identifies. Complexity can be increased by varying the number of words, the length, and the difficulty of the sentence.
- Make the child responsible for remembering birthdates of classmates and birthdates and anniversaries of family members and other relatives. Require him to give you notice when to send a gift or card.
- Play "Furniture Store." After the children cut out pictures of various pieces of furniture from magazines, one child orders a number of articles. The "salesperson" delivers the correct merchandise to the customer.
- Devise other games similar to "Furniture Store" by using pictures of grocery items, restaurant food, toys, clothing, and so forth.
- Ask the child to remember particular items when you take him to the grocery store. Gradually increase the number of items which he is expected to remember. Having him remember things he likes increases the motivation to remember.
- Have the youngster recall events from the morning, the previous day, or the last weekend.
- Ask the child to describe what he wore yesterday, what he had for dinner last night. Requiring the child to focus on the correct order of events or details also aids his sequential memory.
- Ask the child to tell you at the end of the day one bit of information he has heard during the day. Obviously, it is important that you give him attention when he speaks.
- Teach the child to listen, recall, and act out stories and nursery rhymes such as "Old Mother Hubbard." Using "Charades" in this way also aids sequential memory.

76

- Request that the child describe what he got last Christmas and what he did last summer. This, of course, encourages long-term memory.

Tasks for Auditory Sequential Memory (Integration)

- Play "I Went to the Country." The child starts with "I went to the country and I took my shoes." The next person repeats the entire sentence and adds another item, "I went to the country and I took my shoes and my hat." The game continues until one person cannot remember the sequence.
- Say the name of several animals and ask the child to present, in correct sequence, the sounds the animals make.
- Tell the child someone's telephone number you want to remember. After several minutes ask him to repeat it to you. Continue this until he is able to remember it. Ask him to dial the number when you want to call.
- Provide practice in the child's memory for his address, telephone number, and birthdate.
- Have the child remember the names of family members, classmates, school, principal, and teacher.
- Have the child learn simple poems.
- Tell simple jokes and have him repeat them. As he gains ability, increase their length and difficulty.
- Tell sequence stories. The child says "I saw a house." The next person adds a sentence and passes it on until the sequence cannot be remembered.
- Have the child sort pictures according to sounds heard at the beginning, middle, and end of words.

Tasks for Auditory Comprehension (Integration)

The child with problems in this area needs to learn to associate auditory labels with concrete objects, movements, and positions. Any activities which allow this process to occur will be helpful. Start with concrete, familiar words and progress to action nouns and verbs and propositions.

• Encourage picture collecting and picture dictionaries to aid concept development and audio-visual matching skills.

• Have the child categorize and classify the pictures (e.g., "Pick out the pictures of things you can wear and name them").

• Use "See and Stand Cards" by Shick. These are useful in developing conceptualization. The kit contains several large cards which are related to six small cards. The cards encourage the child to spontaneously express himself and discuss the relationship between the cards.

• Play the "I Wish" game. Using a toy box filled with toys, ask the child to fulfill the wish (e.g., "I wish for a toy that floats"). Utilize objects in the room with common color, texture, or function to play games similar to the above (e.g., "I am thinking of things which hold objects." "I am thinking of the color red." "I am thinking of things that are soft").

• Permit the child to trace or to write letters as he sounds them out.

• Allow him to manipulate three dimensional letters to provide a combination of sensory experiences which helps reinforce the auditory skills.

• Play riddle games with the child. Riddles help develop comprehension skills and help the child to understand the connection between detail and function (e.g., "What's black and white and red all over?").

• State a word and have the child name everything that is associated with that word (e.g., "Name everything that you can think of that is blue").

• Provide opportunities for the child to discuss similarities and differences in things (e.g., "How are a church and a band the same?" "Different?").

• Teach the child various proverbs and sayings and discuss the meanings with him.

- Have the child visualize and then draw the scene which the proverb suggests (e.g., "A bird in the hand is worth two in the bush").
- Discuss television commercials and have the child cut pictures from magazines and newspapers which advertise the same product or a common group of products.
- Play scramble word games in which the words in a sentence are scrambled and the child has to arrange them in correct order. These are available commercially or they can be made from magazine clippings.

Tasks for Auditory Expressive Language (Expressive)

- Discuss and then sound out and practice particular sounds which are troublesome to the child.
- Use a tape recorder in which the child may talk, read, sound out words, and so on. Playback is very useful in helping the youngster identify and isolate problem sounds.
- Have the youngster observe himself in a mirror as he attempts to pronounce sounds which are difficult for him. Help him observe and note the way his tongue looks and feels when he does this.
- Provide frequent opportunity for the child to use acquired vocabulary until the language is overlearned and used spontaneously. It is important that the child be given many chances to communicate.
- Make frequent use of "tongue twisters" such as "She sells sea shells by the sea shore" and "Peter Piper picked a peck of pickled peppers."
- Read poetry, interest, and text books to the child. Ask him to read along with you. As you say the words, he says them also. This reinforces correct pronunciation.
- Have the child place his hand on your (or his own) face or throat as you pronounce certain words. This helps him to feel the movement.
- Use word association to help word recall (e.g., pins-needles, black-white, good-bad).

- Show pictures and ask the child to describe what is happening in each picture.
- Have the child explain a particular item in the picture.
- Have the youngster also tell what went on before and after the picture.
- Make use of play telephones, walkie-talkies, puppets, and tape recorders to encourage word and sentence usage.
- Provide the child with correct syntax usage by asking him to repeat the sentence correctly. For example, have him change "I got the ball" to "I have the ball."
- Encourage the child to respond in correct sentences. Use his one- or two-word response in a sentence which paraphrases his meaning.
- Have the child cut out pictures which demonstrate past, present, and future tenses of verbs.

Conclusion

The tasks presented in this chapter are intended to supplement a systematic remedial and developmental educational program for the learning disabled child with auditory problems. Thus the teacher must find ways to integrate these training techniques with the regular activities of the classroom. Although some children will have problems so severe that they can be dealt with only in an individual setting, other children with less debilitating problems can be helped in small-group situations.

Parents also can aid the child in the development of auditory skills. At home, they can supplement the school program. Many of the preceding exercises can be used during play times or when the family is traveling. If they are presented as games, the child is likely to enjoy them while sharpening the auditory facilities so necessary for learning.

At both school and home the activities provide an avenue whereby the child can receive the practice he needs in auditory function. In addition, hopefully he receives attention, support, and encouragement for engaging in learning-related tasks.

8

Specific Learning Disabilities: Hyperactivity Problems

Introduction

The specific learning disabilities which are related to the senses of sight and hearing have been discussed in the preceding chapters. This chapter focuses on the third sense that is used in the learning process—the sense of touch. Certainly the importance of touch in learning is not as crucial as are the senses of sight and hearing. However, the manifestation of learning disorders affected by the touch modality is broader than the mere process of touching. Rather, this modality finds its expression in the motor activity realm; the disability is evident in various physical, psychomotor, and kinetic aspects.

Hyperactivity is the most commonly recognized form of motor disability. Impulsivity, short attention span, and perseveration also are associated with motor activity difficulties, either as separate problems or as subcategories of hyperactivity. **Hyperactivity** is defined as disorganized, disruptive, and unpredictable behavior, usually involving an overreaction to stimuli. Although the particular behaviors of the hyperactive person are not necessarily dysfunctional in and of themselves, the excessive magnitude and degree of behavior do cause difficulties. *The term refers to the child who is usually in motion and whose motion is usually twice the normal speed.* The hyperactive child is simply much more active in a purposeless way than are most children his age. While almost all children are overactive at one time or another, the hyperactive child demonstrates an aimless restlessness, consistent fidgetiness, and excessive movement that is decidedly different from the behavior of the typical child of the same age.

Usually the hyperactive child can sit for only a short time and even when sitting often wiggles and squirms excessively. He may show little patience and may not sit still for television, meals, or stories. He generally has a short attention span and is unable to concentrate on any activity for a reasonable length of time. He frequently talks too much, often on totally irrelevant (to the task) issues. The hyperactive youngster is often very impulsive and tends to blame others when things go wrong. He may be frustrated easily, irritable, and quick to anger—in an unpredictable and explosive way. He usually sleeps less than other children and may even get out of bed and roam around at night.

Needless to say, a youngster who experiences some or all of the above characteristics may well have problems in relating to others and in the learning process. Because of their problems created by poor concentration, these children are prone to failure. Even more serious are children who have hyperactive problems along with either visual or auditory difficulties. Some authors (Meyers and Hammill, 1969) believe that disorders of motor activity usually contribute to the severity of the visual or auditory disability but seldom are themselves the cause of disorders in academic and social learning. This notion suggests that the hyperactivity sits on top of, let's say, the visual perception problem and greatly accentuates the difficulties related to visual learning. Consequently, hyperactivity represents an important consideration in understanding learning disabilities and the children afflicted by them. Next to severe underachievement, hyperactivity is perhaps the adult's most consistent complaint concerning the behavior of the learning disabled child.

Areas of Hyperactivity

There are several specific areas which appear to be involved in hyperactivity. Although each of the problems can exist in a child apart from the hyperactivity syndrome, the hyperactive child usually exhibits one or more of the following problems: short attention span, impulsivity, perseveration, and emotional lability.

Also discussed in this chapter is the issue of hypo-activity—less activity than normal—which is included because of the motor-activity problems which are involved.

The following sections specify some of the specific areas which represent problems to the hyperactive child.

Short Attention Span

It is common for the hyperactive child to experience difficulty in attending to a task for a reasonable length of time. That is, the child is unable to concentrate on one activity for the period of time appropriate for his age and intelligence. He is drawn to irrelevant stimuli in his environment which interfere with social and academic learning situations. For example, Tim is asked to clean the shed. An hour later Dad finds him playing with an old skate. Tim really may have intended to work but became distracted by the possibilities of the skate and consequently forgot what he was supposed to do. Paula begins work on her school assignment. She answers the first question and then begins to listen to noise outside and to play with her pencil. She starts to think about what is for lunch and to daydream about the school field trip tomorrow. Thus she fails to complete her assignment.

Both children initially had the intention to complete the required tasks. The sights and sounds of the environment distracted them. In effect, both children have difficulty attending to the assigned job because they are inefficient in organizing inner and outer stimuli in a way that excludes thoughts and feelings and sights and sounds which are unrelated to the task at hand.

In reference to the child with problems of this sort, Strauss and Kephart (1955) wrote:

> He finds it impossible to engage in any activity in a concentrated fashion, but is always being led aside from the task at hand by stimuli which should remain extraneous but do not. . . . Under these conditions it would be expected that the individual would tend to respond to a variety of extraneous stimuli and lose track of the task at hand. We would describe such behavior as distractibility. [Reprinted with permission. Strauss, A.A., and Kephart, N. *Psychopathology and Education of the Brain-Injured Child, Vol. 2.* New York: Grune and Stratton, 1955, p. 135.]

According to this concept of the hyperactive child, an environment of overstimulation would exaggerate the symptoms of short attention span and distractible behavior. Thus finding ways to minimize the extraneous stimulation should help the child to increase his attention.

Impulsivity

Impulsivity, or poor impulse control, is the imitation of sudden action without sufficient forethought or prudence. Besides having short interest spans, many hyperactive children also have and create problems with their impulsive behaviors. All of us occasionally talk or act before we think. The problem with the learning disabled child is that he appears to do it much of the time and in situations that are most stressful to us. Chris rides his bike across the street without looking for traffic; Larry comments on Aunt Margaret's appearance regardless of the embarrassment it causes.

Children with impulsivity problems seem unable to balance their desire to do a behavior with the consequences of that behavior. That is, the hyperactive child may react to the first element he recognizes in a situation, respond to that element only, and be unable to anticipate the consequences. This quality, of course, may interfere with his need to learn to delay gratification. Even more immediate are the problems connected with poor planning and judgment. The impulsive hyperactive child is more likely than most children to run off in several directions at once. They don't seem to organize their work or their time.

An important aspect of impulsivity has to do with individual differences toward slow or fast decision time. The impulsive child characteristically makes rapid decisions and frequent errors. That child reacts both reflexively and immediately and has great difficulty inhibiting his responses to internal and external stimuli. He acts on the spur of the moment. He rushes into situations which may be potentially dangerous. He blunders into inappropriate decisions. As a result, he receives more than his share of abrasions, cuts, and bruises. He destroys toys and clothes. He is frequently in trouble with siblings, peers, parents, and teachers.

Perseveration

Perseveration refers to the tendency to continue a behavior automatically and often involuntarily. Problems generally arise from the inability of the child to shift with ease from one set, topic, word, or action to another. Perseveration problems may be observed in almost any expressive (motor) behavior such as drawing, painting, reading, writing, and speaking. Gross motor expressive behavior as well as fine motor behavior may be affected. The child who exhibits perseveration may cover an entire page with one color, continue to draw in a circular motion after drawing a circle, or continue to pound a nail after it has been completely embedded.

The child also can perseverate on an emotional response—experience prolonged laughter or crying, for example. To the concerned adult the reaction seems exaggerated. The disequilibrium remains long after the precipitating event is removed. It appears that the controls are rudimentary, and the capacity for critical evaluation is absent.

The child exhibiting perseveration appears to be locked into a repetitive act which continues long after it ceases to be appropriate. The child is unable to alter the focus of his attention. Needless to say, the child tends to adjust poorly to new situations and tends to have difficulty moving to new activities. Such disturbance impedes learning and the process of teaching. It also tends to be upsetting to parents and others.

Emotional Lability

Emotional lability is one of the most frequently mentioned characteristics of children with hyperactive problems. Children with this problem are highstrung, overly sensitive, and fluctuating. They may have quick changes of emotional response from easy manageability to hard-to-control extreme temper. They may be panicked by what seems to be a minimally stressful situation. This mercurial behavioral shift is a frequent concern to adults who must live and work with learning disabled children.

Basically, the learning disabled child is frustrated. Although no child is immune from this situation, the learning disabled child is particularly vulnerable. The following explanations are proposed for the high degree of emotionality exhibited by the learning disabled child.

1. A disturbed pattern of impulses contributes to distortion in behavioral and emotional patterns.
2. Perceptual problems interfere with the child's efforts to make successful contact with the world, which leads to unusual behavior patterns and

misinterpretations of reality.

3. Motor disorders in the child tend to prolong dependency on the parents, particularly the mother.

The child who constantly experiences failure frequently develops anger, hostility, and aggressive behavior. For the learning disabled child, these feelings may find their expression in emotional lability.

The moodswings and cycles lead to unpredictability. Adults report that the child is happy one minute, impossible to get along with the next, that he has good days and bad days. Although all of us experience and express some shifts in mood, the distinctive thing about the hyperactive child is the degree, repetitiveness, and intensity of the shift. Needless to say, parents and teachers are directly affected by this emotional lability of the child.

Hypoactivity

Hypoactivity is the opposite and countercondition to hyperactivity. It is included here as an addendum to our concerns about "hyper" problems in children. **Hypoactivity** is used to describe the child with inadequate motor activity. The hypoactive child seems underactive. It takes him a long time to perform most activities; this often frustrates adults. The comment frequently heard is "He is so slow. He just can't seem to get moving." The child is further described as slow and daydreamy due to his moving, speaking, and thinking at a markedly reduced rate.

Although the hypoactive child appears to be slow responding, he may concurrently have a short interest span, fidgety movements, and be distractible. It is as if the hypoactive child is expending as much energy as his hyperactive counterpart. Even though his body remains in one place, his attention is easily distracted because his thoughts flit from place to place. The lethargic, quiet natures of these children create little disturbance; consequently, the activity problem of the hypoactive child is frequently not recognized. Therefore, the symptom appears only occasionally in case studies of learning disabled children.

Activities for Hyperactivity

Because of the nature of hyperactivity problems, the activities section will have an approach different from that in the auditory and visual chapters. Specific tasks which are designed to remediate the problem appear less helpful with this learning disability. *What is important is the need to create a climate by structuring the environment in such a way to facilitate the hyperactive child's social and academic learning.* Consequently, most of the following tasks provide ways in which the adult may structure the situation—rather than exercises, activities, or games to help the child directly.

Tasks for Short Attention Span

• Require the child to complete specific jobs in a setting with as few auditory and visual distractions as possible.
• Place his desk in the corner of the bedroom (classroom) or some other out-of-the-way location. Keep radio and television off. Keep desk top cleared of everything but the current assignment.
• Provide the structure of time to the task at hand. As much as possible, require that the job be done at the same time every day (e.g., take out the trash as soon as you come home from school every day). Also, provide a specific time limit for the task to be completed (e.g., You have 20 minutes to clear the dishes from the table).
• Become aware of the amount of time the child seems able to tolerate a given task. Try to encourage him every time to increase slightly the amount of time he attends to a task. For example, if the child sits still and reads fairly well for three minutes, encourage him to try for three minutes, 30 seconds. An oven timer is useful for this activity.
• Keep the assignments short enough so that he feels satisfactions and is interested enough to want to continue.

Three 10-minute study periods are generally more productive than one 30-minute period.

• Further structure the assignment activity by allowing the child to come up to the teacher's desk with the completed page. Provide encouragement for completion of each task.

• Read the two chapters (Chapters 12 and 13) on behavioral management in this book. They provide both structure and rewards which have been particularly helpful for hyperactive children. Behavioral approaches, in particular token economies, provide powerful tools with which to strengthen good attending behavior.

Tasks for Impulsivity

• Point out feedback cues from the environment and help the child internalize standards. It may be necessary to adjust the system of feedback so that the child is recognized for partially correct responses.

• Instead of punishing the child, allow him to suffer the logical and natural consequences of his actions. If he rides in traffic without looking, he may not ride his bike again for so long. If the child insults Aunt Margaret, he must apologize to her. Chapter 11 provides additional information related to this procedure.

• When the child interrupts a conversation, require him to wait until a more appropriate time.

• Discuss with the child what one can expect from breaking the rules in playing games.

• Play checkers, "Stratego," or chess and discuss in advance alternate possible moves and their implications.

• Secure the child's cooperation by mutually determining and recognizing goals (e.g., "When we go to visit, what things should you avoid doing? How can I help you do that?"). When you help the child anticipate *how, when, where,* and *why,* you are teaching him to predict events and outcomes.

• Provide firm rules with consequences clearly understood and consistently enforced. Limits should be carefully and explicitly established.

• Routines should be structured with certain times for certain activities (e.g., a certain time for homework, reading, and meals).

• Give the child a monitoring role that requires specific responsible behavior at specified times.

Tasks for Perseveration Problems

• Provide both verbal and nonverbal cues which interrupt the perseveration and aid the child in changing his attention.

• Separate the locations in which particular activities occur. Using various parts of the room facilitates change in task orientation.

• Encourage the child to listen, wait, and then respond appropriately.

• Develop instructional activities which require a variation of response to achieve success.

• Present activities for skills already mastered, but structure them with minor changes.

Tasks for Emotional Lability

• Provide few rules and strictly adhere to them.

• Teach the child to relax. As much as possible, anxiety and tension should be drastically reduced.

• Emphasize an atmosphere of friendliness, order, and helpfulness. A less threatening and more supportive social climate helps to control the emotionality.

• Provide a punching bag, heavy pillows, or big plastic punching toy to hit, kick, or throw. Encourage the child to use this in lieu of a temper tantrum.

• Keep your temper when the child has an outburst. Remain calm and handle it in a quiet, firm manner. Ignoring the lability and focusing on the issue are most helpful.

Activities for Hypoactivity

The Premack Principle, or Grandma's Rule, which is discussed in Chapter 13 is extremely useful. Arrange the desired task so that it precedes an activity that the child enjoys and prefers. When the child does the appropriate task, then he may do the preferred task. This frequently decreases the amount of time required to complete the desired task.

• Recognize individual differences. If your child is a slow mover and a slow doer, he may never change that nature very much. Learn to adjust to it.

• Give the child specific time periods in which to complete a task (e.g., "You have 10 minutes to make your bed"). Provide him supervision to assure that he continues working on the task until it is accomplished.

Conclusion

Evidence suggests that the hyperactive child may eventually outgrow the physiological and temperamental problems which beset him. The problem we have as teachers and as parents is that the hyperactivity causes a lag in the child's learning process. Some of the tasks necessary for educational development are missed. The activities provided earlier in this book should prove helpful for some of these tasks. Good, effective, and creative teaching using a prescriptive format should also help ameliorate the educational problem.

The hyperactive child—indeed, any learning disabled child—may also develop psychological difficulties; he may learn patterns of psychological maladjustment. Parents and teachers must be alert to the emotional and psychological issues that are critical for the learning disabled. The following chapter discusses exactly this point. Subsequent chapters provide strategies for improving the emotional climate of the home and classroom and provide useful guidelines to help the learning disabled. They will be particularly useful for the hyperactive learning disabled.

PART II

PSYCHOLOGICAL PERSPECTIVES

This section is devoted to issues and strategies of a psychological nature. Children who have learning difficulties due to a perceptual problem almost always have concomitant psychological and emotional problems. The adults responsible to and for the child are forced to deal with the emotional problems as well as the educational ones.

The five chapters in this section present psychological strategies which have been helpful in improving classroom and family interactions. Chapter 9 discusses the emotional issues which confront learning disabled children. A procedure for improving self-esteem is also discussed. Chapter 10 deals with a communication model based on the theories of Carl Rogers and Thomas Gordon. Chapter 11 provides a framework for understanding goals of misbehavior and several corrective procedures developed by Alfred Adler and Rudolf Dreikurs. Chapters 12 and 13 comprise behavior modification principles and strategies.

What I have tried to do in this section is to provide

exposure to three seemingly divergent theoretical positions. This reflects an eclectic position, which needs further explanation because of the different ideological systems that support the theories. An eclectic selects concepts taken deliberately from a variety of theoretical positions rather than concepts based on one orientation exclusively. This book reflects the position that a single viewpoint is limiting. Concepts, procedures, and techniques from many sources must be used to best serve the needs of people seeking help.

Teachers and parents are practitioners of psychology. Practitioners are concerned with positive outcomes—with effectiveness. The majority tend to be pragmatists, discarding that which doesn't work and retaining that which does. Each of the approaches suggested here provides a framework which can be used alone if the principles and procedures seem reasonable and are followed by the adult. Since people differ in value systems, need systems, and personality structure, there is likely to be a different response to the approaches. Some individuals respond positively to communication; some, to behavior modification; some, to Adler's ideas.

Another way in which this material can be utilized is to look for ways to integrate the approaches. As a point of fact, there are many more areas of agreement than disagreement between the adherents of the various positions. Apparent differences often are a matter of terminology and style rather than real substance. The differences that do exist are most often related not to critical issues but superficial ones. It is possible to implement procedures from one theory without violating the basic position of another theory.

Most of the adherents of each of the theories would agree that communication with children is important. To have more productive and satisfying relationships, individuals in classrooms and families need to communicate more fully. The information and skills adapted from Gordon are designed to provide this.

Many teachers and parents, while agreeing that communication is important, want models for understanding the child. The section on goals of misbehavior provides that model along with corrective procedures which supplement the communication skills. Flowing from the Adlerian position are the notions of logical and natural consequences, useful in themselves and a natural lead into the principles of behavior modification. Graphically, this flow is represented in Figure 2.

Figure 2   Pragmatic Integration of Psychological Principles

Communication Skills
↓
Goals of Misbehavior
↓
Logical and Natural Consequences
↓
Principles of Behavior Modification

Pragmatic Integration of Psychological Principles

What is called for is an integration of those principles which logically and pragmatically are consistent. Beyond that, one must seek the selective use of elements which are most appropriate for the situation and the child.

The eclectic position taken here does not represent a new theory of working with children but rather a pragmatic position for applying different approaches. One of the implicit assumptions of this present position is that many theoretical approaches have the potential for beneficial application to children, teacher, and parent problems. More effective interaction can be best achieved by accepting an eclectic theoretical-technical position. The next few chapters particularly support the viewpoint that eclecticism is required and cannot be sacrificed for isolated allegiance to any one position.

9
Attending to Emotional Needs of Learning Disabled Children

Introduction

The issue of emotional lability which was discussed in the last chapter as a coordinate of hyperactivity needs to be further defined. While the hyperactive syndrome does indeed include emotional problems, the issue of emotional problems is an important consideration for every learning disabled child and the adults close to him.

In the past the problems presented by learning disabled children were considered psychological and emotional in origin. If a child did not take out the garbage, he was rebelling. If the child seemed unable to recognize certain words, his anxiety was causing him problems. If the child rushed to and fro in an impulsive frenzy, he had poor impulse control and was exhibiting his fear. There are, in fact, a fairly large number of people—professional and lay, teachers and parents—who still consider the symptoms and behaviors described in this text to be entirely due to emotional factors.

Many children have similar symptoms which, indeed, are due to psychological, not physical processes. We know, for instance, that some children do express their rebellion by not taking out the garbage, that some children have problems with reading because their anxiety does block their perception, that some children do have poor impulse control and act out their fear. There is, however, an increasing body of research which supports a different explanation for such response in learning disabled children. As discussed earlier, the learning disabled child probably has difficulty in learning due to subtle physiological causes. That is, the *primary* problems associated with not learning are *not psychological* or *emotional in origin*.

On the other hand, virtually every learning disabled child has some emotional difficulty. This disturbance can range from mild to quite severe, but it is almost always present. Consider the situation. The learning disabled child has at least average intelligence, but there is a discrepancy between what he is expected to be able to do and what he is actually achieving. He is bright enough to recognize his own failure. This undoubtedly creates some emotional conflicts. In many cases, parents have not understood the hidden handicap and have expected and demanded behaviors which were unattainable. The negative response in the child that has resulted probably has created emotional problems. Teachers have expected and demanded performance which the child has been unable to accomplish; this too has created emotional problems.

Children are total beings. They have cognitive, physical, and emotional components to their personalities. An effective teacher and a good parent attend to the physical areas, the intellectual development, and the psychological needs of the child. Up to this point, we have stressed the intellectual areas with some attention to the physical components involved in the learning process. To do justice to the child, we must consider his psychological functioning.

Categories of Emotional Problems

A child who feels particularly bad about himself probably cannot reach his learning potential. He engages in behavior that is negative, inappropriate (to the task at hand), and self-defeating. It is the responsibility of significant adults—parents and teachers—to modify the situation and/or their responses to situations so that the emotional problems of this learning disabled child can be better resolved.

What are these emotional problems? They appear to fall within two broad categories. The first category is the negative affect which frequently builds up within the learning disabled child. This negative affect seems to be expressed most often either as anger, hostility, and antagonism, or as fear and anxiety. The other broad area of emotional difficulty is the negative self-esteem which is common with learning disabled children.

Negative Affect

If the learning disabled child is angry, he may express it in hostile and aggressive ways. This creates problems for us because although the child's anger is understandable, we frequently react as if it were not. The child may be angry at the unfair expectations placed upon him. He may be angry at his inability to "measure up." He may be angry at adults who act as if something is wrong with him and yet pretend that there is not. He may be angry at the constant burden of improving all his weaknesses.

Teachers and parents who may be the target of the child's anger must first of all recognize the source within the child. Once having recognized this, a helpful stance is to *not personalize the attacks of hostility*. The child has a right to his anger; it is probably an appropriate expression. Outlets, such as pounding clay, using a punching bag, or running around the block or gym, may help the child appropriately channel the anger and aggression.

If the child is experiencing fear, he is likely to be

passive. The fear of failure in academic and social areas leads the learning disabled child to reject even the notion of trying. His interactions with siblings, peers, or adults may be characterized by withdrawn, nonexpressive behavior. Allowing opportunity for the child to express his fears and hurts without defensiveness on the part of the adult is helpful with the passive child.

Many psychologists believe that a child's greatest fear is that of being unloved and abandoned by his parents. With the stress that a learning disabled child creates on those around him, he frequently gets messages that he is unlovable, so he may believe he can be abandoned. A child should never be threatened with abandonment—even in jest. Adults must reassure the child of his worth.

Our society discourages the expression of negative feelings—particularly anger—toward the object of those feelings. As a consequence, many children cannot express their feelings to anyone. They need to be provided with opportunities to express feelings. Individual, family, or group counseling has proved to be helpful. In this situation, children find that they can discuss their negative emotions and they are not alone in their feelings. They can be helped to realize that those feelings are quite normal.

Low Self-Esteem

A number of people who have worked with learning disabled children suggest that low self-esteem is a central problem. Indeed, a child who faces the defeats common to learning disabled children might well devalue himself. It has been found that low self-esteem is characterized by significant underachievement. That is, the child with a low self-concept does less well than expected when only his ability is taken into account (Shaw and Alves, 1963). Apparently achievement and self-esteem interact. The low self-esteem produces lower performance, which in turn reduces the self-esteem, which in turn leads to even lower performance. Because of the learning problems they face, learning disabled children are particularly vulnerable to this vicious cycle.

There also is evidence that low self-esteem inhibits the person's participation in learning activities. Maw and Maw (1970) discovered that high-curiosity boys tend to have more positive self-concepts than a comparison group of low-curiosity boys. If the more curious child is more likely to seek out information and to involve himself in learning tasks, the negative self-concept of the learning disabled child may indeed inhibit this behavior and thus contribute to poorer performance.

One way to counteract negative self-esteem is to involve the child in learning experiences and tasks which can provide some degree of success. Praise for this success is most important. Many of the activities included in this book will hopefully provide just such an opportunity for success and subsequent praise. The problem of self-esteem is such a pervasive one for the learning disabled child that adults significant to the child must focus particular attention on the issue.

Five Steps for Improving Self-Concept

Felker (1974) suggests five steps which are believed to be useful in improving self-concept. The five steps are: (1) significant adults must praise themselves, (2) children need to evaluate their behavior realistically, (3) children need to set reasonable goals, (4) children need to praise themselves, and (5) children need to praise others.

Teachers who utilized these steps were found to improve the self-concept scores for their students. Their pupils were also less anxious and experienced less failure. Felker emphasizes that his system is an *action program* which involves helping the child in specific ways to improve his self-esteem.

Step 1: Adults must praise themselves. Children learn from models. If we want the learning disabled child to learn to feel better about himself, we have to demonstrate concrete ways which will do this. By hearing significant adults praise themselves, children will be more prone to praise

100

themselves. This self-praise will improve their attitude about themselves.

It is important to begin self-praise by complimenting your work and then move to praising your personal qualities. Ginott (1965) suggests that dealing with accomplishment rather than personal qualities is less threatening and consequently easier to do. It is important, however, at some point to focus on more personal qualities so that the child can see that those areas more centrally related to the person's being also are worthy of praise.

Step 2: Children need to evaluate their behavior realistically. The feelings an individual has about himself to a great extent are derived from his attitudes about his own behavior. If a person is consistently evaluating himself against an unrealistic standard, he is bound to perceive that most of his efforts are failures. This issue is of particular importance to learning disabled children because of their special handicap that interferes with their learning and behavioral processes. If the child perceives that his efforts are failures, self-praise and self-reinforcement are inappropriate. Self-reinforcement is appropriate only when it follows success or progress toward success. If the child is evaluating himself from an unrealistic base, he probably will have low self-esteem.

Some evaluations of behavior and performance may indeed be negative and *realistic*. But a realistically negative evaluation should provide a basis for change which will increase positive performance and thus positive evaluation. The learning disabled child frequently works below grade level. The grade level standard—especially in areas affected directly by the disability—may be totally inappropriate for a particular child. It is unrealistic to expect that level of performance.

A parenthetical but pertinent point is the continuing practice of teachers to correct papers by citing the number of *wrong* rather than the number *right*. Most children continue to miss 3 words on their spelling test; they do not get 17 words correct. Parents contribute their share by remembering the number of times Billy spilled his milk but not the number of times he *did not* spill his milk. With the learning disabled child, the problems are increased because he learns to think of himself negatively and the negative view is based on unrealistic or bias evaluations. While one-half of a glass of water is both half-empty and half-full, it is important for a learning disabled child to think of it as half-full. This should help him move toward realistic evaluations in positive terms.

Another important aspect of realistic evaluations of performance and behavior is that the evaluation be based on past performance. That is, the present evaluation should be in relation to the past accomplishments of the individual. As mentioned earlier, too frequently learning disabled children are compared to grade level or some other reference group. To the child with a handicap, this must be enormously discouraging and defeating. If the youngster's present behavior or performance is tied to his own earlier achievement, then his self-evaluation can have a more realistic basis.

Step 3: Children need to set reasonable goals. Research has suggested that people with negative self-esteem tend to set their goals either unrealistically high or unrealistically low. Either standard creates a no-win situation. If the child sets an unreasonably high goal, he doesn't attain the goal and doesn't succeed. Thus, he is a failure and his self-concept becomes more negative. If the child sets an unreasonably low goal, he does attain the goal, but it is not an accomplishment anyway so he doesn't succeed. Thus, he is a failure and his self-concept becomes more negative. In either situation the child loses.

As in realistic evaluation, the notion of reasonable goals must be based on the individual's past attainment of goals. Information as to success and failure in achieving prior goals must be utilized in determining present goals. If the child with an auditory memory problem could remember and comply with one command last week, then setting the goal of remembering and complying with two commands this week is appropriate. It doesn't make any sense to work for remembering four, five, or six commands. Learning is accomplished in small, methodical steps. Goals should reflect this.

The criterion-referenced teaching procedures which are currently being proposed (see Block and Anderson, 1975) in a number of teacher-training programs provide an excellent example of realistic goal setting. The notion is that all youngsters are able to master content. Temporal differences rather than achievement differences may not be as threatening. That is, having to learn a concept or skill *within a limited time* is considerably *more* threatening than simply having to learn the concept or skill. In mastery teaching, the child is tested on content, and his deficiencies are noted. He is provided instruction calculated to remediate the deficiency. He is re-tested to determine the effects of instruction and to point up his deficiencies. Thus the child who learns at his own pace is considered as an individual. Testing and teaching are designed to reflect his past learning experiences. Goals are realistic and reasonable.

A final characteristic of effective goal setting is the notion of an *end-goal* as well as a *step-goal*. Often, children are not satisfied with the attainment of small units which form the learning process. The step-goals which allow the individual to get from point A to point Z are viewed as not important enough to bother with. On the other hand, the end goal is so far away that the child has difficulty staying with the task long enough to reward himself. Identifying the end-goal and then discussing the step-goals in relation to the end-goal helps bridge the gap. Having short-range, attainable goals allows the child to see that he is working on something that is possible. It also increases the opportunity for external reinforcement and, more important, allows self-reinforcement and self-praise.

Step 4: Children need to praise themselves. Early learning of humans is dependent upon significant others. Gradually, however, the results of early learning become internalized and begin to direct and influence the experience of the individual. In the matter of self-esteem, the child must become his own evaluator and reinforcer. Consequently, he must develop the skills and the habits necessary to give himself verbal praise when it is appropriate. While this idea holds true for all children, it is particularly important for the learning disabled child. Verbal self-rewards operate in a circular manner. Behavior in which the child has engaged is reinforced and is thus likely to occur again. Positive statements are reinforced by the successful behavior; one becomes reinforcing of the other.

Self-esteem is basically internal. The perceptions, ideas, and attitudes about the self are stated aloud and in an internal dialogue. Part of the task of improving self-esteem is to develop a new set of verbal self-references. Felker (1974, p. 86) points out:

> Teaching the child to engage in self-praise is not only teaching him to reinforce his behavior, it is teaching him a new set of self-referent ideas. To say, "I did well on that," not only reinforces what it was that was done, it attaches to "I" the label "well-doer." It is this aspect of self-praise that is the most important for self-concept. People maintain their ideas, including the ideas which they have about themselves, with a system of words. A set of positive words and phrases which the child learns to apply to himself is a powerful mechanism for self-esteem. [Reprinted with permission. Felker, D.W. *Building Positive Self-Concepts.* Minneapolis: Burgess, 1974.]

Given the social norms which operate against positive self-communication, significant adults must encourage and actively teach verbal self-reinforcement and self-praise. This can be done initially by cultivating a system of group praise and then moving on to individual self-praise. When all the family members complete a work task—say cleaning the garage or weeding the yard—statements such as, "Boy, the yard looks good. We do good work, don't we?"

are very appropriate. In the classroom statements such as, "We did a good job in arithmetic today, didn't we?" encourage group praise.

Eventually, the adult needs to find ways to help the individual child praise himself. One way to elicit this is to ask questions rather than, or in addition to, give adult praise. When the child brings home a completed paper, a question, "Do you think you did a good job?" elicits the reinforcement from the child. It may also be helpful to follow his self-praise statement with your own praise such as, "I think you did a neat job, too. You really should pat yourself on the back." The emphasis, however, is upon the child and his self-referent verbal reinforcement.

Step 5: Children need to praise others. Research has indicated that praise of others and self-praise are positively related. Apparently, praising is a learned skill which is applied in similar situations whether to oneself or to others. Thus, this step is important as a tool to accentuate step number four. That is, by learning to praise others, the child can more easily learn to praise himself. There is another extremely important consideration. Praise of others brings praise in return. People like to be reinforced, and they tend to respond in pleasant ways.

The significant adult must be concerned with two processes in encouraging children to praise others. She must teach the child how to give praise to others; she also must teach the child to receive praise from others. Although these constitute two separate functions in reality, the process can be accomplished simultaneously. This is obviously evident if giving praise back is emphasized as one way of receiving praise.

Some parents and teachers have fallen into the habit of always pointing out incorrect behavior and mistakes, ignoring good behavior. If this is the situation, the model which the child has is contrary to this step. The adult would do well to observe and then modify his own behavior if this is the case. Providing a good model by noticing and praising positive behavior is one way to teach praise. Open discussion including sharing good feelings about others also is a way to encourage praise of others. Encouraging children to ignore the failure or inappropriate responses is another way. Finally, helping the child to be specific, give examples, and focus on particular behavior can create a climate and the skill for learning to praise.

In teaching the child to receive praise, the adult needs to encourage him to acknowledge the positive contact. Sometimes a simple "thank you" is sufficient; sometimes the contact can be acknowledged by giving praise back. Another important consideration is to help the receiving child avoid disclaiming or discounting the praise. In the encounter groups which I facilitate, the theme of "the little voice" often arises. "The little voice" is usually activated when a person says something nice, positive, or praising to another in the group. "The little voice" says, "If you knew how rotten (or bad or nasty or unworthy) I really am, you wouldn't be able to say that about me." Most of us have little voices, although they say different things to each of us. The effect is to discount the positive stroke and to perpetuate the negative self-esteem. Children's little voices also are there, but they tend to be more verbal about them. This acts as a discouraging force to the praise giver.

By following these five steps, teachers and parents can increase the feelings of self-worth in the learning disabled child. As self-esteem increases, the behavior and performance of the child will improve.

Conclusion

The learning disabled child indeed must cope with emotional problems. There are procedures which can be used by parents and by teachers to aid him in his adjustment. In addition to the procedures covered in this chapter, three areas—adult-child communication, under-standing underlying purpose of behavior, and child-management approaches—have been most helpful in minimizing emotional reactions of children. The following four chapters deal specifically with these psychological strategies.

10

Communication with the Learning Disabled Child: Gordon's Approach

Introduction
Influence of the Parents

Effective family relationships are not just the result of the particular mix of personalities who happen to live in the same house, nor are they the result of individual characteristics of the children in the family. Of course, these factors have an effect, but much of the child's behavior is the direct result of parental behavior. For example, parents who do not share power with their children, who constantly reprimand them using sarcasm and ridicule, and who create a competitive rather than a cooperative climate are encouraging certain kinds of behavior in their youngsters. Parents of this type probably will have more than the usual degree of negative family interactions.

On the other hand, parents who create a warm and supportive climate by honestly sharing power and by making a place for everyone encourage their youngsters to receive satisfaction from more positive interaction with siblings and the parents themselves. Open and effective communication allows parents to create this positive climate. This chapter specifically deals with the improvement of family communication. While geared primarily to parents, the material considered in this chapter is also most appropriate for teachers.

Perhaps parents can't do a lot to change the whole world, but the parents and the family do affect the child's world. They are the nucleus of it. Parents do determine to a great extent whether that world will be gloomy or sunny, ugly or pleasant, harsh or accepting. Communication is the single largest factor determining the relationships at home and subsequent events in the world at large. If you know in your heart that you are not communicating effectively in your family, it is time to begin to do so. As the poster says, "Today is the first day of the rest of your life."

Previous Condemnation of Parents

Previously, professionals have viewed the parents' input as negative. They have tended to develop the approach that parents have been the cause of problem children. The problem child has been considered the "symptom" of pathological parent behaviors and attitudes. Parents were blamed for all of the difficulties of their children. Many professionals were of the belief that parents ought to know better, or at least change their attitudes and actions at the professionals' requests. Parents were regarded as inevitable but unpleasant factors in working with children. This intolerance for parents fostered the wide-spread use of one-word diagnoses to describe parental attitudes—rejecting, overprotective, coercive, compulsive, and so forth. It seems quite likely that these labels were reflective of the irritation which the professional experienced toward parents whose attitudes seemed to interfere with attempts to help the child. As

Fred Allen once joked, "These days it almost seems as if parenthood is a disease" (Langford and Olson, 1972, p. 95).

A Change in Attitude Toward Parents

Recently, however, there has been a growing group of professionals who have emphasized a very different view of parents. Emphasizing the need to educate parents, some professionals, such as Gordon (1970), Dreikurs and Grey (1970), and Becker (1971), have adapted systems of therapy which can be effectively utilized by parents to improve the family interaction. These and other writers have developed principles which support parents' involvement in the treatment of their own children and which facilitate parents' interactional abilities in nonproblem homes. Similar programs have used teachers in the classroom system as the focus of involvement. Gordon, in particular, has focused on the development of communication training for parents, following the thrust of Carl Rogers.

Teaching Parents to Create a Therapeutic Relationship

Rogers and Stevens (1971) state that the reason for the therapeutic effectiveness of practitioners of sharply differing psychotherapeutic orientations is that " . . . they bring to the helping relationship certain attitudinal ingredients" (p. 4). The various elements of these attitudes, which can be used by parents, will be described briefly.

Elements of a Therapeutic Relationship

The first ingredient is empathy. This involves the ability to experience an accurate empathetic understanding of another person's private world. It further means being able to communicate some of this understanding to another. This is also described as the ability to sense another person's inner world of private feelings as if it were your own, without losing the "as if" quality.

The second ingredient is that of genuineness. This refers to a person's willingness to be himself, not denying himself. It is being open to his own feelings and the feelings that a relationship arouses. It also is being able to communicate these feelings; that is, to meet another individual on a person-to-person basis.

The third ingredient is that of positive regard or warmth. This attitude involves caring for a person in a nonpossessive way, experiencing a warm, positive, acceptant attitude toward a person, prizing him, and being willing to allow him the freedom to experience his real feelings of the particular moment. It is a caring stance which has strength and yet is not demanding.

Rogers (1961) states that a person need not be a professional to experience these attitudinal components. He says that "the best parents show them in abundance, while others do not" (p. 86). Consequently, it appears that these parents are able to develop therapeutic relationships with their children.

The Value of a Therapeutic Relationship

A child who experiences therapeutic human relationships with his parent expands not only himself but the self of the parent. The child feels respected and loved by the parent; the parent feels respected and loved by the child. Such reciprocal experiences do not have to occur in the constant statement of "I love you" or in the physical embrace of parent and child. Therapeutic human experiences can occur between child and parent at bedtime or mealtime, while reading, walking, playing, or singing. Any experience which brings the child and the parent into positive direct and human contact with each other can be growth producing for both.

Resolution of Conflict

When such therapeutic human encounters have been experienced, conflicts between child and parent can be much more easily resolved because the love which exists between the two persons rises to the surface in the process of resolving the conflict (Ginott, 1965). Both are able to internalize the dimensions of their own idiosyncratic tendencies and how they are perceived by others. They also are better able to become more sensitive and appreciative of the equally human frailties of the person with whom they are in conflict. In addition, the conflict cannot long endure because it is softened by the basic attitudes which both share.

Conflicts between the child and parent create more permanent psychological damage when there are few mutually shared previous therapeutic experiences to cushion the present conflict.

A Parent Training Model

Unfortunately, in our society most mothers and fathers have few opportunities to learn creative and effective ways of dealing with problems. Gordon has directed a portion of his time to the development of a model for parent training called Parent Effectiveness Training, or P.E.T. (Gordon, 1970). The course has been taken by thousands of parents in the United States and abroad. Designed originally for parents of problem children, it now attracts parents of well-functioning children as well as potential parents. The program focuses upon teaching parents specific skills that will keep channels of communication open between them and their children. These include listening skills and communication techniques for conflict resolution. The underlying philosophy is one of teaching the establishment and maintenance of an effective "total relationship with a child, in any and all circumstances" (Gordon, 1970, p. 5). Gordon states, "We have demonstrated in this exciting program that with a certain kind of special training, many parents can greatly increase their effectiveness in parenthood" (Gordon, 1970, p. 2).

Specific Communication Notions

The following discussion is organized around several of Gordon's (1970) concepts with material being included from other sources to expand upon the theme.

Problem Ownership

Most writers acknowledge that in any relationship, problems will definitely arise. Gordon (1970) has developed a way of looking at these problems which attaches responsibility or "ownership" to them. "Who owns the problem" is of critical importance; the adult must be able to decipher the situation because the answer suggests different responses and different modes of communication. If the adult "owns" the problem, a particular set of skills is employed. If the child "owns" the problem, another set of skills is used. If the adult and child mutually "own" the problem, still another set of skills is brought to bear. The first critical job of the adult, then, is to define just who does own the problem.

When the child owns the problem, he is blocked in satisfying one of his needs. His behavior in no way interferes with satisfaction of the parent's needs. When the parent owns the problem, the child is satisfying his needs and by so doing interferes with the satisfaction of the parent's needs. The relationship is said to "own" the problem when both the adult and the child are directly affected and are in conflict about the situation.

To determine who owns the problem, it is suggested that the adult ask herself who will reap the results of the problem in a tangible way. Or the adult may ask herself this question, "Do the results of the problem directly and/or tangibly affect my ability to meet my own needs?" If so, the adult owns the problem. If not, it is probably the child's problem. Or if the parent finds both he and the child are directly affected by the results of the problem, it is owned mutually or owned "by the relationship." Thus, whoever reaps the results of the problem owns the problem.

Active Listening

Active listening is employed if the adult determines that the child owns the problem. The purpose of active listening is to communicate a deep sense of acceptance and understanding to the child. It is expected that in this atmosphere of respect and acceptance the child will fully express his thoughts and emotions regarding his problem and choose a course of action with which he (the child) is satisfied.

To achieve this purpose, the adult listens with empathy to the child's feelings about the problem. Communication involves more than just the words exchanged between people. The emotional and affective dimension of the communicative process is reflected in eye contact, body movement, and tone of voice. The adult employs a technique of listening which allows the child to confirm that the adult does understand what he's feeling and is "with" him. When the child talks more about his feelings, amplifies his thoughts and feelings, goes from surface to in-depth feeling, or fully expresses the feelings that are at the heart of the problem, the adult knows that the child is moving toward the desired goals of being freed from the emotion of the problem, understanding it, and therefore being able to deal with it on his own. When the child begins to suggest his own solutions after active listening has occurred, it is a sign to the adult that the child has approached the goal of solving his own problem. At times active listening only helps the child accept an unchangeable situation, or it gives him a chance to get his feelings out and experience genuine acceptance for having them.

Active listening is accomplished by the adult who goes out of herself in search of significant cues emitted by the child. The active listener is receptive to all nuances of the

114

child's personality and expression and truly seeks to understand the child's message. The active listener, however, goes even further than this; she realizes that the proof of good listening lies in the way she responds to the child. She must demonstrate accurate empathy (Rogers, 1961) since it is essential to growthful interpersonal relations. Active listening requires getting inside the child, viewing the world through his eyes, and communicating understanding of him. Essentially, then, the adult must respond to the words the child uses as well as to the feelings which lie behind the words. The following transcripts demonstrate the skill.

Child: I hate school. I wish I didn't have to go anymore.

Adult: Sounds like things aren't going too well and that you would like to be doing something else (active listening).

Child: Yeah. I hate all the homework we have to do.

Adult: You have a lot of homework and that frustrates you.

Child: Yeah, I better get busy.

Another example of active listening is presented in the following adult-child interaction:

Child: I don't see why we have to do this stuff.

Adult: You don't like this assignment, do you?

Child: No, it seems dumb.

Adult: You can't see much meaning for you in this.

Child: Yeah, I don't like oral reports. How come I can't do a written one.

Adult: You're more comfortable writing than you are speaking to a group.

Child: I . . . I'm not much good talking to a class.

Adult: You'd rather do what you can do well than try something where you feel uncomfortable.

Child: Yeah, cause I always mess up when I talk to the group.

Adult: What can I do to help?

Child: Maybe you could listen to my report.

In both of the above instances, the adult listened to the child, sensed a message beyond the words, and communicated that understanding to the child.

Detrimental to active listening is the parent's frequent manipulation of it to control the child. Parents also too frequently begin active listening at first to open the door but subsequently slam it shut because of lack of time or because their own attitudes get in the way. Interference also occurs when parents simply parrot back a message to the child without trying to understand it or when they send back a message which is devoid of any empathy.

Active listening is not in order at all times. Sometimes a child just wants information. Then, giving him information is the appropriate response. When there is lack of time because of the press of other duties, trying active listening is not useful. Most of all, active listening is inappropriate when the parent "owns" the problem.

Sending "I-Messages"

When the adult determines that he owns the problem, that is, his needs are directly and tangibly being affected, there are several things he can do. He can modify the environment, himself, or the child directly.

Often, with younger children, changing the environment will promote a modification of the child's behavior and, thus, solve the adult's problem. Such changes may include simplifying or enriching the environment as well as substituting one activity for another. It is helpful to prepare older children for changes and to help them plan ahead for such shifts in the environment or coming events.

To limit serious conflicts, a parent can change himself. If a parent can grow to accept himself and satisfy his own needs, he doesn't have to achieve gratification through his children to feel he is a person of worth. If a parent can feel his children are separate from himself, he is bound to be more accepting of them. He can better accept his children by letting them be themselves and by liking them

116

all the time, not just when they behave as the kind of children he values. Of course, this implies liking the children although some of their behavior is unlikable.

Finally, a person can seek to modify the child directly. Sometimes this is accomplished by spanking or some other corporal punishment; sometimes it is accomplished by other types of punishment. The trouble with punishment is that it is often not effective and leads to avoidance or escape. Even if punishment does stop the annoying behavior, it leads the child to build resentment against the punisher, and the child's self-esteem is negatively affected. Consequently, most adults stop short of direct physical punishment, choosing verbal punishment instead. Frequently, this takes the form of put-down or derogatory statements which are often sent in "you-messages" (i.e., "*you* are a pest"; "*you* are lazy"; "*you* are a bad person"). Unfortunately, messages of this nature are worse in some ways than physical punishment. Besides lowering the child's self-esteem, they also communicate only part of the true message and are thus inexact.

In contrast to the ineffective "you-message," a simple "I-message" is the most useful tool in confronting the child. In an "**I-message**" the adult clearly expresses to the child her problem and her feelings about the problem, while letting the child know that she, the adult, "owns" the problem. When the adult shares her feelings with the child, the child is often willing to modify his behavior. An "I-message" is less apt to provoke rebellion and resistance, and it places the responsibility upon the child for changing his behavior. The following examples demonstrate the contrast between "you-messages" and "I-messages."

You-message: "You didn't do your chores this morning. You are really a lazy kid."

I-message: "I'm angry because you didn't do your chores, and I had to do them after you left."

Comment: The focus is on the problem of the chores and not on the character or personality of the child. The parent's feelings of annoyance and anger are not openly shared in the you-message; the anger is clear in the I-message.

You-message: "You are a pest. You always interrupt your mother and I when we are talking."

I-message: "I get frustrated with you because mother and I can never finish a conversation without your interruption."

Comment: The "I-message" communicates the parent's feelings, puts responsibility on the child for his behavior, and does not lower the child's self-esteem.

By sending an "I-message," the adult anticipates that the child will understand the adult's problem, respect his needs, and therefore discontinue acting in a negative way. Frequently, an "I-message" is adequate for modifying the child's behavior. Occasionally it is necessary to follow the "I-message" with a change in the environment. For example, after communicating frustration at being interrupted, the father could require the child to leave the room so that he and mother might finish their conversation. Modifying the parent's own attitude by allowing the child to participate in the conversation or by talking with him at a later time may be necessary for less conflict. Sometimes mutual problem solving is necessary.

Mutual Problem Solving

Frequently, conflicts arise between adults and children because both are tangibly affected by an interaction. Mutual problem solving is employed when it is determined that the needs of both the child and the adult are being blocked by a problem.

Too often solutions to problems and conflicts occur in one of two ways, both of which are based on a power struggle. In method 1, the adult wins and the child loses; in method 2, the child wins and the adult loses. In both situations, one person goes away feeling defeated and usually angry. In method 1, the child is denied opportunities to develop self-discipline and inner-directed responsible behavior. Method 2 is ineffective because it teaches children to manipulate others, encouraging them to be selfish, which will lead to difficulty in social adjustments.

Gordon (1970) suggests the "no-lose" method to be used whenever adult and child encounter a conflict-of-needs situation. Essentially, the adult requests that both participate in a mutual exploration for a solution to the conflict. A solution which is acceptable to both thus creates a "no-lose" situation for both the adult and the child. Gordon's six problem-solving steps are outlined as follows.

1. *Identify and define the conflict.* It is important to determine if the disagreement is actually over the issue at hand. Perhaps the conflict is really over a different matter, and the current problem reflects another concern. Both parent and child need to be clear on the conflict.
2. *Generate possible solutions.* Both adult and child need to indicate as many alternative solutions as possible.
3. *Evaluate the alternative solutions.* Once the partners have mentioned potential solutions, their effectiveness needs to be critically evaluated. Both adult and child have to decide which solutions they can live with.
4. *Decide on and get commitments for the most acceptable solution.* Both must agree to commit themselves to the solution, possibly by modifying their own behavior.
5. *Work out ways of implementing the solution.* The adult and child must decide who is going to do what and when it is to be done. Both must agree to the practical, concrete issues which are involved.
6. *Follow up and evaluate how the solution worked.* After some time has lapsed, it is important to review the solution to determine the satisfaction with it.

This method avoids the detrimental side-effects of other approaches. By engaging the child in the process of mutually solving the problem, both are able to fulfill their needs. Thus, conflicts can be resolved in a healthy manner which builds a relationship that is mutually satisfying, friendly, deep, and intimate.

Effective parenting derives from a philosophy in which respect for the child is uppermost. This means respecting individuality, uniqueness, complexity, idiosyncratic potential, and capacity for making choices. This philosophy must be expressed in effective communication. Effective communication between adult and child is expressed via cognitive, affective, verbal, and nonverbal modes. Useful parenting requires open communication that is encouraged and facilitated by a nonthreatening atmosphere. The preceding skills help create this climate. Because of the importance of communication in family relationships, the following exercise is proposed.

An Experiential Exercise

The following exercise developed by Rogers (1961) has been frequently employed in human relations training and in various classroom situations. The exercise is difficult and challenging, but generally people value the learning experience involved and derive genuine satisfaction from it.

Two people, in this case an adult and child, are asked to discuss a topic on which they hold differing views. Each is allowed to say whatever she likes under one condition: before voicing views, each person must restate the feelings and ideas expressed by the other person to that person's satisfaction. The assumption is that if I can tell you what you felt and said, then I heard and understood you. If I cannot, either you did not make yourself sufficiently clear, or I placed obstacles in the way. Thus the exercise motivates the listener to truly concentrate on what is being expressed and motivates the speaker to clarify his communication.

As the feelings of the participants begin to rise in the discussion, it may be more difficult to obey the rule. At times tempers reach such a high point that a neutral person is required. Forming a triad, the neutral person restates to each participant's satisfaction what he has felt and said before the next participant is allowed to speak.

Conclusion

It is important that both adult and child be able to speak and be heard by the other. Learning to provide an atmosphere in which each can release feelings and ideas without interference from the other leads to truly genuine communication and to more effective parenting.

11

Understanding Goals of Misbehavior: An Adlerian Approach

Introduction

In addition to the need to communicate with the child, it is equally important that the adult have some understanding of the purpose and goals underlying the child's behavior. One of the best schemes for understanding the child's behavior is Adler's notion of purposive behavior and the subsequent goals of misbehavior.

The point of view contained in this chapter is based on the concept of social interest contributed by the Viennese psychiatrist Alfred Adler. Dr. Rudolf Dreikurs has become the foremost interpreter of Adlerian psychology to the American situation, introducing Adler's ideas through his Community Child Guidance Centers now functioning in Chicago and elsewhere. Much of the material presented in this chapter is derived from Dreikurs' work (Dreikurs, 1957, 1958, 1964; Dinkmeyer and Dreikurs, 1963; Dreikurs, Grunwald, and Pepper, 1971).

Adler points out that every human being is born with the potentiality of social interest. **Social interest** implies that the feeling of belonging and the ability to cooperate, participate, and contribute are crucial to the common welfare in the family and in the classroom. Those things that increase the child's feelings of belonging, as well as those which give equal social status and significance, increase his social interest. Conversely, whatever makes the child feel inadequate, inferior, or humiliated decreases his social interest. Given the learning and adjustment problems facing the learning disabled child, the parent and teacher must be sensitive to the issues involved in social interest.

Human life is social life. Social feelings are necessary for good mental health. The child learns effective or ineffective social behavior through his interrelations with family members and school personnel. However, all human beings have an innate tendency toward social interests. Through learning social behavior, a person adapts his interests to those of society. By bringing his private interests into agreement with general human interests he has the best chance for success. That is, the organism must learn to accomplish tasks and overcome obstacles in a way that not only benefits himself but all those around him.

The constructive approach for increasing the child's social interest is the maintenance of order without conflict within the family and the classroom. This is of fundamental importance. In learning to accept order willingly, the child begins to cooperate with others and thus increases his social interest. It is essential that the atmosphere be one of *mutual* respect, tolerance for mistakes and failures, and kindness. Equally important, however, are firmness, regularity, and the maintenance of order.

The maintenance of order, however, relies on a true understanding of the underlying purpose of the child's misbehavior. In addition to the individual being conceived as a social being, his actions are considered to have purpose. Adler states that all behavior is **purposive**. There is a purpose in a child's every action. The child's place in the group is his basic intention. In an unacceptable way, the misbehaving child mistakenly seeks to gain social acceptance. Social position has been achieved by the well-adjusted child; he meets requirements of the group by making useful contributions to it.

Purpose is not the same as *cause*. **Cause** implies the desire to dredge through the past to identify what event, person, or situation causes the child to behave in his present fashion. Purposiveness, on the other hand, reflects the goal orientation which corresponds to the child's perceptions of reality. In this context, children perform behaviors which they feel will gain known desirable consequences or help them avoid punishing consequences. Thus the purpose of the behavior is currently operating in the present; the cause of behavior exists in the past. The purposiveness of behavior can be changed, modified, and redirected; the cause of behavior is frequently non-reversible and thus of minimal use to the child, his parent, or his teacher.

Defining Goals of Misbehavior

Since all children have behavior which is purposive, it should be possible to classify the goals so that parents and teachers can better understand the purpose. This is, indeed, the case. Dreikurs suggests that a child's misbehavior may have one or more of four goals. The four goals are (1) attention-getting mechanisms (AGM) (The child wants service and attention); (2) power (The child wants to be boss); (3) revenge (The child desires to hurt others); (4) inadequacy or assumed disability (The child wants to be left alone).

In striving for these goals, the child considers his actions to be logical, even though he is usually unaware of the underlying purpose of the behavior. Striving for these goals also suggests discouragement because a misbehaving child often is a discouraged child. His discouragement elicits misbehavior, which the child believes will gain him significance. He may seek attention, or he may attempt to show his power; he may direct himself toward revenge or demonstrate his inadequacy—all designed to get special exemption. His behavior, regardless of the goal he adopts, results from the belief that this is the most effective way to function in the group. Understanding the goals of misbehavior is most helpful for understanding the learning disabled child. Consequently, a further description of the four goals follows.

Attention-Getting Mechanisms (AGM)

Most children exhibit AGM. The child believes he is unable to become part of the group through any useful contributions he can make. Thus he seeks importance and inclusion through attention. Initially, he may seek his attention through socially acceptable means. If this proves ineffective, he tries any method by which he can be noticed.

There is a vast array of behaviors that are negative and attention getting. The *purpose* is to engage the adult. The goal underlying the acts is to get adults to serve and pay attention to the child. The adult's intervention can continue to reinforce the child's method for getting attention. The child would rather be punished than ignored. Doesn't one frequently see learning disabled children who behave in this way?

While attention getting is most often connected with negative behaviors, the very cooperative behavior of children may result from a desire for special attention. It is difficult to distinguish between behavior which stems from a genuine feeling for belonging and willingness to contribute and that which primarily is a plea for attention. If the child seems to be *using the pay off* for his behavior of being better than the other children, he needs to realize that adult reinforcement is not ultimately necessary to prove his worth. Satisfaction can be derived for the act of cooperation rather than the favorable response it evokes.

This is important as one thinks of the siblings and classmates of the learning disabled child who may attain attention to the detriment of the learning disabled child. If a "successful" AGM child finds value in being best, the learning disabled child might well find value in being worst. Research and clinical observation suggest that this is indeed so. Families and classrooms develop reciprocal relationships with children playing roles which exist because of counterroles.

Power

With the goal of power, the child appears to believe that his worth is based on his ability to dominate, control, and manipulate the adult. The child refuses to be commanded; he does what he desires and thus demonstrates that he has control and power.

If the adult responds to the power struggle and succeeds in showing more power to force compliance, the child becomes even more convinced of the value of power. Even more important, the child's goal is not so much to win the struggle as it is to get the adult involved. When the adult joins the battle, the child wins a significant victory. The child, of course, would prefer to get his way. But regardless of the end result, the child has satisfied his need to engage the adult—the real reason behind the behavior. Thus, the child usually does score a victory each time he defeats a command or an order although often he does not win the struggle.

Learning disabled children make use of power to assert their feelings of worth. If an individual has difficulty learning, he may well attempt to demonstrate to himself and the world that he, indeed, does have power over others. This is highlighted by the potential interface of the specific learning disability and the struggle for power. For example, the youngster with an auditory memory problem may be told before leaving for school that he is to take out the trash when he returns home. When he "forgets" to comply, the adult is unsure whether he actually forgot because of the memory disability or because he is attempting to exert power. Ways of dealing with this are presented later in this chapter.

Revenge

The child who opts for the goal of revenge is extremely discouraged, and he is considered to pose the greatest problem. Severity of the symptoms in young children by no means permits an assumption of deeper personality disturbance. Only beginning with the period of adolescence do these symptoms take on pathological significance. The child whose goal is revenge has perceived that he can no longer maintain his position by attention or by power. He is able to be significant by hurting others. He concludes essentially that "I can't be liked; I don't have power, but I can be hated." His violent antagonism provides his place in the group.

Generally, this goal is sought only after a long series of discouragements have convinced the child of his utter lack of belonging. He has reached the conclusion that everyone is against him and his only way of gaining recognition is to retaliate against adults for the way he feels he has been treated. Once the child takes this position for himself, he is able to evoke treatment from adults which justifies the continuation of the revenge.

This goal is sometimes present in learning disabled children. Frequently, it is the result of an unrecognized handicap and subsequent unrealistic expectations and pressures established by significant adults. Due to the learning disability, the child may be unable to accomplish a particular task. Assuming negative motives, the parent punishes the "lack of trying." The child is hurt by the encounter and wants to hurt back. If these scenes are repeated enough times, the goal of revenge becomes established.

Assumed Disability

The child who is fulfilling the goal of assumed disability expresses himself by his inadequacy. He expects failure and he uses his disability to escape participation. It is as if the child is so convinced of his being an utter failure that he does not even try any more. The child wants to be left alone, and as long as nothing is expected of him, he can still appear to be a member of the group. By hiding behind a display of real and imagined inferiority, the child believes that he can avoid even more embarrassing and humiliating experiences. The important aspect of this goal is that if the child feels inadequate and incapable of functioning, he will not try, regardless of whether his deficiency is real or merely assumed.

This goal poses serious problems for parents and teachers who work with learning disabled children. The disability is the result of a real difficulty, probably physiological, which the child has encountered. The child quickly realizes that the disability is the most effective way of keeping adults involved with him. Thus, it is convenient to continue the disability even when it no longer exists. Too often adults fail to distinguish between the actual disability and the lack of ability that is *assumed* by the child.

Using Clues To Identify the Child's Goals

The Child's Pursuit

In most instances, the child is in the pursuit of one of the four goals. Sometimes he has not determined his goal orientation and we find him in between attention and power or in between power and revenge. Some children seem able to switch from one goal to another and actually operate toward all four of them, to the distress of parents and teachers. Sometimes the child may have one goal at school, another goal with his peers, and still another at home.

To understand the child's actions, one has to see them as a whole, not as emanating solely from the child in one situation, but as being part of the total situation in which the child, his teachers, friends, and parents all cooperate to give meaning to what he does. In each event, one has to recognize the child's goal and deal with it.

The Adult's Feelings
and Child's Reaction To Reprimand

Fortunately, there are some useful clues which are helpful in determining the direction of the goal. The first clue is the feeling engendered in the adult toward the misbehaving child. As the child behaves in such a way to receive the fruits of the goal, parents and teachers are themselves emotionally affected by the child's action. Their emotional response is a powerful key to understanding the purposiveness of the child's behavior. The second important clue is the child's behavioral reaction to the adult's reprimand. The child responds differently to corrections according to the goal of misbehavior that is in operation. By observing this behavior, one can make better judgments about the purposiveness of the goal. Because of the importance of these clues, let us examine them more closely.

1. If the adult's initial feeling is that of annoyance, irritation, or surface anger, then the goal is probably *attention-getting*. The child reacts to correction by temporarily stopping his disturbing action. Essentially the scolding, coaxing, helping, reminding, and so forth provide the needed attention. Thus the behavior stops—*temporarily*.

2. If the adult's anger goes beyond mere annoyance and the anger is coupled with feelings of being challenged and provoked, then the goal is probably to gain *power*. Further clues are the sentences which run through the adult's mind at this point: "I'll show you who's boss around here." "I'll make him

do it." "You can't get away with that." When the adult behaves according to these sentences, the child actually intensifies his actions.

3. If the adult feels intense anger with an underlying response of hurt and shock, then the goal is *revenge*. The sentences are "How could he possibly do that to me?" "This kid is just nasty and unlovable." "How could he be so vicious and cruel?" If the adult behavior is motivated by his anger response, then the youngster will try other ways to get even. He may seem to want to be disliked and hated. If the adult responds with hurt, sadness, and perhaps tears, the child might actually smile.

4. If the adult feels despair and frustration and even feels that the child is beyond help, the goal is *assumed disability*. Because of the nature of this goal, there usually is no reprimand. The child responds generally with great passivity and communicates with his behavior that he feels helpless, discouraged, and that it is no use to try.

In most cases we as adults feel exactly what the child intends us to feel. It is mandatory that we reflect upon the initial feelings that the child's misbehavior arouses within us. In disturbing situations we feel particular emotions because the interaction has triggered them. If we continue to react merely according to what we feel, we help the child fulfill his mistaken goal. It is important to ask during moments of provocation: "What does he expect from me?" "What do I feel?" The direction of these feelings reveals what the child is seeking from you. Once we have some understanding of what the child is seeking, we can then avoid our more inappropriate reactions and strengthen our efforts toward more constructive ends.

Corrective Procedures

The schema we have been discussing implies various corrective procedures for each of the goals. As we come to better understand a child, we can use these procedures. The corrective procedures involve behaving in a different way in response to the child as well as interpreting the child's goals to him. This last point needs further elaboration.

No one is fully aware of why he behaves as he does. Only a few of our intentions reach the conscious level. When one asks a child why he did something wrong, he probably can't answer because he doesn't know. If the child does give an explanation, it usually is a rationalization. The child usually is not aware of his own motive. The sensitive adult can help him become aware by disclosing the goal of his disturbance to him. This confrontation with his goals can be the first step toward a change. This is not to say that the adult tells the child what he is—aggressive, lazy, disturbing. Even if true, these labels have no meaning for the child. Rather, the adult confronts the child with the goals of the behavior—with the intentions underlying the behavior. The alternative of continuing with the behavior or not is then possible, because with understanding of his goals, the child then can decide whether he wishes to continue. All improvements and corrections imply helping the child see alternatives. By interpreting the child's goals to him, the adult provides alternatives. "Could it be ... " questions are most useful for this. All questions must be asked in a friendly nonjudgmental way and not at times of conflict. Moving through each of the goals, the following section contains possible interpretative questions and corrective procedures that help the child progress to a more appropriate and useful behavior.

Corrective Procedures for AGM

• Help the child understand the attention-getting aspects of his behavior by asking "could it be" questions. "Could it be that you want me to do special things for you? ... that you want to keep me busy with you? ... that you want me to notice you?"

131

- Ignore this misbehaving child.
- Give attention at pleasant times when the child is not making a bid for it.
- Recognize that punishing, giving service, coaxing, and scolding are forms of attention and serve to perpetuate the negative behavior.

Corrective Procedures for Power

- Utilize "could it be" questions to help the child discover the purposiveness of his behavior. "Could it be that you want to be boss? . . . that you want to get me to do what you want? . . . that you want to show me that you can do what you want and no one can stop you?"
- Recognize and admit to yourself and to the child that the child does have power.
- Withdraw or do not engage in conflict. That is, "take your sail out of his wind."
- Act; don't talk.
- Establish equality, with willingness to negotiate as many issues as you can.
- Redirect the child's efforts into constructive pathways. This can be accomplished by enlisting the child's co-operation, appealing for her help, and giving her responsibility.

Corrective Procedures for Revenge

- Identify the *revenge* goals with "could it be" questions. "Could it be that you want to get even? . . . that you want to hurt me? . . . the other children?"
- Avoid punishment and, especially, retaliations.
- Maintain order with minimum amount of restraint. Use group encouragement.
- Win the child and try to convince him that he is liked. In the classroom enlist a "buddy" for him—a peer who will provide support and friendship.
- Do not become hurt or show your hurt.
- Take time and effort to help child. Learn to change

your own behavior so that you will not respond to old provocations.
- Consider professional help such as counseling.

Corrective Procedures for Assumed Disability

- Use "could it be" questions to reveal the goal of inadequacy. "Could it be that you feel stupid and don't want people to know? . . . that you want to be left alone? . . . that you want to give up?"
- Show encouragement and recognize that it may take a long time. Show faith in child's ability.
- Avoid discouragement yourself. Don't give up.
- Provide success for child in areas where he can succeed. Work on strengthening areas of deficiency.

Encouragement as a Corrective Procedure

Encouragement is a corrective procedure which cuts across each of the goals of misbehavior. Because of its importance, it is given special attention at this time.

Encouragement means increasing the sense of worth and strength of a child. Really effective encouragement is expressed not only in a set of behaviors, although proper behaviors are important and can be learned. Effective encouragement rests on attitudes of acceptance and support. These attitudes are appreciated by children and must be developed in adults who work with them. In a relationship of sincerity and frankness with the adult and the child facing the issues as equals, the element of encouragement is present. Encouragement includes also the recognition of the child's strengths and assets—his *actual*, not his potential, strengths and assets.

Too often children are exposed to a sequence of discouraging experiences. Deliberate encouragement is essential to counteract them. The child does not believe in his ability to succeed with useful means and misbehaves because he is discouraged. Encouragement implies the adult's faith in the child. It communicates to him the adult's belief in his strength and ability, not in his potentiality. Unless the adult has faith in the child *as he is*, the encouragement is not communicated to him.

In efforts to encourage children, one must be sensitive to the child's response. The accent must move to "How can I help the total situation?" and away from "What am I?" Anything one does which perpetuates the child's false image of himself is discouraging. What one does to help the child understand that he is a part of the functioning unit, that he can participate, cooperate, and contribute within the total situation is encouragement. *It is important that the child learns that he is good enough as he is.*

Natural and Logical Consequences as Corrective Procedures

Allowing the child to experience natural and logical consequences constitutes two corrective procedures which can be applied to counteract the various goals of misbehavior. Like encouragement, these techniques help adults improve their relationships with the child.

Using natural consequences allows the reality of the situation to provide order. In applying this technique, one relies heavily on the safety principle: no one will willingly do what he believes is harmful to himself. The reason that people do so many things which ultimately harm themselves is that at a given moment they believe mistakenly that a particular course of action is the best or at least the safest to attain what they want.

When natural consequences are allowed to occur, the child experiences the unpleasant results of his own actions. Thus he can well understand reality and its demands. Interfering with the consequences of a disturbed order deprives the child of corrective experiences and hinders his learning to respect order and reality. Only in moments of *real* danger is it necessary to save the child from the natural consequences of his disturbing behaviors.

The logical consequences premise is much the same as

natural consequences, but the result is more or less arranged by the adult. Essentially, the "punishment (consequence) fits the crime" and evolves from the misbehavior. Thus, the adult strives to strengthen the *relationship* between the misbehavior and the consequence. Children can see quickly the connection between their own behavior and the result, if it is properly presented. The child, then, experiences the unpleasant result of his own actions.

Conclusion

With a firm and definite knowledge of the goals of misbehavior and with an understanding of the principles of encouragement and logical and natural consequences, the adult can help create an environment which is safe and productive for the learning disabled child. Some children present behaviors which require a more systematic procedure to help them with their functioning. The following two chapters based on behavioral principles help provide this systematic procedure.

12

Improving Behavior of the Learning Disabled Child

Introduction

Family and school problems do not "just happen." Like everything else, they have causes. Family problems often are caused by the inappropriate, undesirable behavior of one or more of the children. Similar situations are present in the classroom. Child-management problems continue to influence the teaching process and to be a major source of frustration for teachers. Behavior modification, a set of applied procedures derived directly from B.F. Skinner (1953, 1971), provides tools for parents and teachers to assist children.

It is now generally accepted that the vast majority of human behaviors are learned and are developed as a result of a person interacting with his environment (Krumboltz and Krumboltz, 1972; Bandura, 1969; Krumboltz and Thoresen, 1969; Skinner, 1953; 1971). By and large, a child *learns* to be a particular kind of person. This learning comes about mainly through interacting with fellow human beings who constitute or provide a principle source of rewards, punishment, and motivation. Both desirable and undesirable behavior have been learned. Consequently, if the undesirable behavior has been learned, then it can be unlearned. In the family situation, the parents are in a critical position to help the child replace problem behaviors with desirable ones. In school, the teacher fulfills that function. The primary aim of this chapter is to provide the parent and teacher a capsule of recent techniques and ideas of behavior modification most applicable to effective child management. All of the approaches and techniques presented have been beneficial to both "problem" and "nonproblem" children. These techniques are especially appropriate and useful for helping ameliorate the special problems of the learning disabled child.

Behavioral Principles
Four Ways To Modify Behavior

There are essentially four ways in which the adult can influence and modify behavior. First, the adult can *shape* or teach a child a brand new behavior which he has never done before. Second, the adult can *increase* or strengthen a behavior believed to be good or pleasing, but which the child doesn't exhibit often enough. Third, the adult can *maintain* or continue an existing behavior of a child which is good or pleasing to the adult. Finally, the adult can *decrease* or weaken a behavior which is felt to be undesirable and which happens too frequently.

Prior to discussing how behavior can be shaped, increased, maintained, or decreased, it is necessary to cover defining, measuring, and recording the behavior in a meaningful way. While necessary as a preliminary step in a child-management plan, defining and recording also have potential for producing some benefits in modifying the child's behavior.

Describing Behavior

Satisfactory, acceptable behavior usually includes

more than the usually vague dictate the adult issues for it. Frequently, the child is told to "Behave yourself." Usually this means to act appropriately or to be polite. However, the child is still behaving when he is inappropriate or impolite. **Behavior** refers to any activity which an individual does. Behavior is larger than *correct* behavior or good manners.

It is important to think precisely about the behavior which one hears and sees. "Mark has been a bad boy" is not a very precise or adequate description of undesirable behavior. The listener does not know what led to the statement. It may even be that Mark himself does not know which of his behaviors led to that evaluation. "Mark left home without asking permission, and then he played with matches" does describe specifically what behaviors created the problem.

How would one describe the child who is always interrupting? First, label the behavior that is a concern. Here, it is "interrupting" behavior. The label needs to be defined within the context of its occurrence; for example, "speaking to the adult without permission while the adult is carrying on a conversation." One has to be careful that the terminology, even in the definition, is clear and can be understood. It is important that everyone concerned, including and particularly the child, know what is meant. For instance, in the above example of interrupting, just what does "permission" mean? A person gives permission in different ways. The adult may say the child's name, gesture toward him, or look at him with eyebrows raised in a questioning manner. The important thing is to know precisely what is included and to communicate that definition to the child.

Measuring and Recording Behavior

By observing exactly what the child does and how often he does it, one can then decide whether the behavior must be decreased or increased in frequency. By communicating the rules clearly to the child, one improves the chances of success. To estimate success, it is necessary to measure the behavior. That is, to evaluate the success of behavior modification, one must measure the behavior before and after the intervention.

The primary reasons for measuring and recording behavior are to establish the degree (frequency, duration, etc.) and contextual conditions of its occurrence. For additional information on these aspects of measuring and recording behavior, the reader is referred to Becker (1971), Krumboltz and Krumboltz (1972), and Patterson (1975). The measurement should be recorded since it is difficult to recall when and how often a particular behavior has occurred. If one describes a child's behavior as "constantly running around," the description is not meant literally. What is meant is taken differently by various people. "Running around" and "constantly" are both terms which are probably interpreted differently by many. Measuring and recording can be used to show accurately how often something occurred. If parents and teachers continue to use terms like "constantly running around" without measuring the behavior in some way, then a change in the behavior stands little chance of being noticed and responded to positively. To carry an illustration to an extreme, if the child sits and rests for half a minute, would the adult admit that there has been improvement? Probably not. On the other hand, truly significant changes in children's behavior are sometimes not noticed by parents and teachers partly because the change has occurred gradually but often because the adult has only a vague understanding of when and how often the original behavior occurred. If the behavior has been measured and recorded, the parent will have an objective indicator of frequency with which to compare change.

Another advantage of counting the behavior is the potential for self-monitoring. Such a technique emphasizes self-control because the child himself can set up conditions in his environment to bring about specific behaviors in himself. Self-monitoring is a simple application of behavioral control. The technique consists of the child's keeping a record or being made aware of the record of the frequency in which he engages in the behavior to be controlled. The technique provides immediate feedback, and the child becomes more aware of his own behavior and its consequences. This helps him to bring it under his control.

Table 1 Wall Chart for Recording Daily Chores

Days	Bed made	Toys picked up	Clothes picked up	Room dusted
Sunday				
Monday				
Tuesday				
Wednesday				
Thursday				
Friday				
Saturday				

For example, a parent is trying to help the child clean up his bedroom before school. Rather than continually questioning, yelling, and/or nagging the child to do this, the parent would do better to provide a simple wall chart with the days of the week along the side and the tasks to be completed across the top. This can provide the youngster and the adult with a clear concrete record of the activities. Table 1 provides an example of a wall chart with activities the child is expected to complete. For younger children, pictures can help communicate the words. After the child has finished the task, he or the parent can check off the appropriate square. A similar chart at school also can help the child. Sometimes, the simple act of counting and recording the behavior helps to move the behavior in a more positive direction. More often, however, the adult needs to provide more tangible reinforcement if the child is to modify his behavior.

Positive Reinforcement

An extremely powerful tool in helping an individual accomplish most activities is the notion of positive reinforcement. The basic principle underlying **positive reinforcement** is to *arrange for an immediate reward after the correct performance of a behavior.* Thus the goal of modifying behavior is accomplished by altering consequences. This technique involves the determination of these consequences or reinforcers and applying them when a desired behavior is approximated.

Another important principle to consider in the use of positive reinforcement is to *always include a verbal reinforcer —encouragement, recognization, and praise* along with the tangible reward. This provides the child with additional reinforcement and sets the stage for withdrawing the candy, toys, and other artificial reinforcers later. Ultimately, a good behavioral program will allow the child to function with only intermittent social reinforcement. Prior to this, concrete rewards are necessary.

A child's reinforcers can be determined by carefully observing his behavior. Each person has a personal preference of reinforcing items which one can rank from most to least important. While money and candy are reinforcers for most children, observation and inquiry are usually necessary to specify a specific list of reinforcers for a particular child. A reinforcement hierarchy or "menu" is useful to the adult in the selection of an appropriate consequence.

The reinforcement menu works like a food menu.

Find out all those things a specific child considers pleasurable and acceptable. Make a list of priorities—a hierarchy —from the most to the least important. The child looks over the "menu" and picks out what he wants to have or do. The child must then engage in what you want him to do before he can have or do what he has picked. Experience with many children under varied situations has established certain kinds of events as frequently effective reinforcers. These include:

> words of praise
> recognition and attention
> candy, fruit, nuts, popcorn
> opportunities to observe certain events
> opportunities to participate in valued activities

Table 2 is an example of two reinforcement "menus" for a 9-year-old boy. The items at the top of the list indicate those activities or objects which are most important and which thus serve as the greatest reinforcers. The right-hand list represents the school-related activities or objects; the left, home-related reinforcers.

Table 2   Reinforcement "Menus" for 9-Year-Old Boy

Home Menu	School Menu
Going on camping trip	Having extra minute of recess
Watching basketball game	
Eating ice cream	Having free reading time
Shopping for toys	Playing "Scrabble"
Playing with match box cars	Working on bulletin board
Watching T.V.	Eating popcorn and nuts

Items are listed in descending order; that is, the strongest reinforcers are at the top of the lists.

Many privileges that previously were considered free (i.e., shopping, television, free reading time) can be included in a behavior-management system. The parent or teacher does not have to search for or make up new rewards. Previously reinforcing events and objects can be used to increase desirable behavior.

Letting the youngster develop his own menu can reveal unusual reinforcement items. One child enrolled in a special school for learning disabled youngsters had "washing the school bus" at the top of his list. His reinforcement system involved a token economy (discussed in the next chapter). When he collected enough tokens, he turned them in for the (to him) privilege of washing the bus.

Punishment

The discussion up to this point has focused on only one of the general types of reinforcement schedules used to modify behavior. This "positive schedule of reinforcement" has been demonstrated to change behaviors in a relatively rapid and durable fashion. Another type is an "aversive schedule of reinforcement." It is characterized by such reinforcers as threats, withdrawal of privileges, confinement, physical punishment, ridicule, and so forth. It generally is acknowledged that behavior changes promoted by the latter kind of schedule tend to be relatively temporary and limited. It may be necessary and useful to use punishment in two situations. When the child's safety is in jeopardy, punishment may be entirely appropriate to insure the child's welfare. Punishment also may be necessary when the alternate (desirable) behavior cannot compete with the undesirable behavior. For example, the child does not come right home from school even though he is told to do so. The undesirable behavior of not coming home is being positively reinforced by the play he accomplishes with his friends. That activity is more powerful than coming home to do his chores. Consequently, punishing him when he doesn't come home, along with rewarding him when he does, may be necessary to accomplish the desired goal.

Even though punishment has many limitations to its usefulness, it is still most often used by adults to control children. Because of its widespread use, it merits further discussion here. Punishment alone is generally less than effective for several reasons. For one thing, it simply pushes down or represses the undesirable behavior so that despite the punishment, the behavior recurs whenever the opportunity presents itself. In other words, punishment does not permanently change the motivation or desire to engage in an undesired behavior. The exception to this principle is extremely severe punishment which is very effective in stopping a behavior. If one punishes hard enough and severely enough, the behavior will stop. However, severe punishment has undesirable side effects. For one thing, it sets up a poor relationship between adult and child so that the adult is not seen as a loving, nurturant person. Thus, he cannot be an effective reinforcer for the child when he uses reinforcement to train him. In effect the adult becomes enemy and adversary and loses most of his effectiveness.

As mentioned earlier, punishment also creates undesirable side effects of anxiety, escape, and avoidance behaviors which, in the end, can be more harmful and undesirable than the original behavior being punished. Finally, if physical punishment is used, it becomes a model for aggressive behavior for the child. If he is hit, he will hit in other situations, copying the aggressive behavior.

In actual practice, the type of schedule used to modify behavior is usually mixed: positive reinforcement to increase or maintain desirable behaviors; aversive reinforcement (punishment) to eliminate undesirable behavior. The key to modifying behavior lies in which of these two is given the major emphasis.

Extinction

A principle which has proved to be just as effective as

punishment in eliminating undesirable behavior is the notion of extinction. **Extinction** is the withholding of reinforcement which has previously been contingent upon a behavior. When a behavior is never reinforced, it will decrease in strength and eventually disappear. To stop a child from acting in a particular way, one may arrange conditions so that he receives no pay off following the undesired behavior. For example, four-year-old Paula would occasionally throw a temper tantrum when not given a cookie. By completely ignoring the crying, foot stamping, and yelling, her parents were able to extinguish the temper tantrum. Because other people in the situation deliberately or unintentionally reinforce the undesirable behavior, one must frequently involve them—grand-parents, playmates, brothers and sisters—to terminate all sources of reinforcement. In the above example, Paula's brothers and sister also were asked to ignore her. In the classroom the teacher must be concerned with this point because even though she stops her reinforcement, the misbehavior may be maintained by the comments, laughter, and encouragement of the other children. To achieve extinction, *all* reinforcement must cease.

When behavior no longer results in reinforcement, the individual generally will accelerate the magnitude and/or the frequency of the behavior in an attempt to produce the reinforcer. This is an extremely important point to remember: with a behavior we are trying to eliminate by extinction, *the response rate may temporarily increase after the start of extinction.* Paula's initial reaction to being ignored during and after her tantrum was to cry and yell louder and more often than before. In effect, things get worse before they get better.

How rapidly a behavior is decreased depends on the previous reinforcement history of the child for that behavior. If the child has been intermittently reinforced (that is, sometimes rewarded, sometimes ignored) for a long period, it will take a long time to extinguish the behavior. The problem, of course, is that most behaviors learned in our environment have been maintained by inconsistent, and thus intermittent, reinforcement. It takes consistent and patient nonreinforcement of the behavior to eliminate it by extinction.

Shaping New Behaviors

New behaviors can be shaped through reinforcement of small steps. **Shaping** is using approximations or steps to a desired goal. When a child is required to learn a new behavior, it is important to start small and work up. The adult must not wait until the child completes the whole process to reward him. When a behavior is selected as a goal, all the responses which are steps to that goal are reinforced and all other responses are not reinforced. To illustrate, a child who fights with his siblings can be rewarded for going a full day without a fight (or even part of a day, if the fighting behavior is severe), then two days, then five days, until it appears he has learned new nonaggressive ways of relating to brothers and sisters. If the fighting is particularly persistent, it may be necessary to start with extremely small steps. Perhaps reward initially for one hour of nonfighting play, then two hours, then a morning, afternoon, evening—start small.

Another example of shaping behavior usually occurs when teaching a child to do a variety of tasks. When Ben is requested to make his bed and he has seldom or never before done that chore, it becomes important to work for gradual improvement. The adult would be wise to break down the task into smaller, easier skills which can be learned one at a time. By reinforcing the child for accomplishing each small skill, the adult can gradually help the child master the total behavior. Learning disabled children, particularly, experience difficulties because they frequently have not mastered the skills necessary for performing the more complicated behaviors expected of them. The helpful adult attempts to identify exactly what preliminary skills a child needs to learn a more complex

146

behavior and then reinforces the series of small improvements which are moving toward the desired behavior. The adult should reward small steps of improvement.

Contingency Management

Another concept which is absolutely essential in understanding behavior modification principles is that of contingency management. Contingency means the consequences of an event are made dependent upon whether the event occurs. For example, telling a child he may have an ice cream cone only if he behaves means that ice cream is contingent upon good behavior. This notion is a very simple and straightforward concept that all of us deal with in a variety of ways during our daily lives. Failure to understand the importance of rewarding or punishing on contingency of the target behavior is, however, commonplace and can utterly destroy the learning of desirable behavior. For example, the child who cleans up his room and then is punished for not minding his father during the previous day is not likely to clean up his room again. Thus, the child is taught not to clean up his room. Likewise, the child who bugs his mother until she buys him a toy is actually rewarded and reinforced for his bugging behavior. He *is taught* to bug.

Conclusion

The attempt in this chapter has been to highlight some of the behavioral principles which affect the desirable and undesirable behavior of children. If children can be taught to behave in more desirable ways, then the adults are fulfilling part of their responsibility.

Because of the importance of behavioral principles and because of the usefulness of contingency management in modifying child behavior, the following chapter will deal with two applications of contingency management which extend behavioral principles. These are the Premack Principle, or "Grandma's rule," and the token economy.

13

The Premack Principle and the Token Economy: Applied Behavioral Approaches

Introduction

To be useful to parents and teachers, behavioral principles must be applied in simple yet effective ways. This chapter deals with two relatively simple and effective approaches which allow rapid implementation of behavioral laws, promoting more desirable behavior. Essentially, the Premack Principle and the token economy are procedures by which behaviors can be changed in specified ways. When an adult knows how to apply these procedures, she knows how to change behavior. Adults who use these procedures generally report that they concomitantly are able to become more loving and positive in interactions with their children. Clear instructions and appropriate consequences replace nagging, yelling, and shouting.

The Premack Principle, or Grandma's Rule
Essence of the Principle

Since this is not the place to review Premack's work,

suffice it to say that he and others are finding considerable laboratory support for the extremely simple notion that has become known as the Premack Principle. The Premack Principle states: "For any pair of responses, the more probable one will reinforce the less probable one" (Premack, 1965, p. 132). This principle, which actually is as old as child-rearing itself, is described by Becker (1971) as "Grandma's Rule." This rule is expressed in such comments as: "You can have dessert after you eat your spinach," or "After you take out the trash, you can watch T.V." Becker summarizes the principle as first you work, then you play. The more probable response (playing) is a reinforcer for the less probable response of working. Thus, the reward for the work is the play.

The application of Premack's Principle is very straightforward. The adult simply notices which behaviors are reinforcing responses. She then permits this behavior to occur only after the behavior she wishes to reinforce has occurred. Interestingly enough, there is very little problem in finding things which may act as reinforcing responses. Homme and his coworkers (Homme, 1966) applied this principle in the pre-school in which they were involved, observing that most of the activities the children engaged in, when given the opportunity, were running and screaming. Homme simply allowed the children to do that behavior *after* they had first performed predetermined tasks which were deemed desirable. Essentially, the running and screaming became approved behaviors and served to increase the amount of time the children spent doing what the teachers had planned.

The procedure for the adult to follow can be summarized in this way: *Observe what behavior is at a high probability at the moment, then inform the child that he can do more of it if he will do a small amount of lower probability behavior first.* The adult needs to adapt to the stress situation by using, rather than being annoyed by, the high probability behaviors. They can be used to reinforce other less probable behaviors which are in need of strengthening.

For example, a child is seated at the table, breakfast is served, and the family is eating. The child, however, plays with his napkin instead of eating. The typical way in which this problem is solved is obvious: "Eat your breakfast! Stop playing with your napkin!" Another way to solve the problem is to notice that playing with the napkin is a high-frequency behavior and can be used by "Grandma's Rule" to reinforce eating which is the less probable behavior. When the situation is viewed in this way, the adult says, "Eat one bite of egg, then play with your napkin some more." Although it may be startling to observers, the latter method works. Instead of having an emotional scene with both child and adult upset, the Premack procedure has the child cooperating in a gamelike atmosphere.

The beauty of the Premack Principle for the adult is that to decide what can be used to reinforce children, one only needs to observe what the child chooses to do when given the opportunity. This activity is then used as the reinforcer. The following list provides some additional examples of successful application of the Premack Principle.

> Pick up the room before you go out to play.
> Do your homework before you have friends in the house.
> Do the dishes before you watch television.
> Read the assignment before you go to recess.
> Find your mittens and then you can have some pie.
> Clean your desk before we have the game.
> Take your bath and then you can have milk and cookies.
> When the floor is vacuumed, then we will go to the game.

In each of these examples the child is required to do what the adult wants before he gets to do what he wants. From this arrangement of the less preferred activity coming before the more preferred one, the child is taught to carry out his responsibilities.

Guidelines for Using
Grandma's Rule (Premack Principle)

Although the application of "Grandma's Rule" is a simple procedure, there are several aspects of it which are critical. If they are not instituted, the procedure may fail. Although these critical aspects were mentioned in the preceding discussion of basic behavioral principles (Chapter 12), their importance demands a systematic and specific treatment here. These items are specifically important to Premack's Principle as well as important in most behavioral procedures.

Item 1: Initial performances should specify and reward small portions of the desired behavior. One does not expect, for example, that a new employee be rewarded only for expert job performance at the beginning. The job is broken down into small tasks that are learned separately. In using "Grandma's Rule" (or any behavioral system), the adult should request that the child accomplish simple-to-perform, small approximations of the desired behavior, at least initially. If the child is not accustomed to responsibility for keeping his room clean, the Premack Principle expressed by "Clean your room and you can go outside to play" may not be effective. A better approach would be to break down the total task into subtasks with a reinforcing behavior attached to each one. Table 3 shows one such arrangement.

Table 3   Breaking Up the Total Behavior of Cleaning a Room Into Its Parts

Pick up your clothes (leads to) →	30 minutes of play time
Dust the furniture (leads to) →	30 minutes of play time
Make the bed (leads to) →	30 minutes of play time
Vacuum the floor (leads to) →	30 minutes of play time

Of course, the child must be able to accomplish each of the subtasks. For a younger child or for a learning disabled child with visual-motor coordination problems, the tasks associated with making the bed also may need to be separated and rewarded. The key is using small, easy steps that lead to the end behavior.

Item 2: Reinforce frequently with small amounts. Rather than providing a few large rewards, it is more effective to give small but frequent reinforcement. Suppose a child has a great deal of homework to accomplish over a long weekend. Providing systematic work periods followed by short periods of reinforcing activities is more productive than using a big reinforcer after it is all done. Like Item 1, this point is particularly important early in the program.

Item 3: Reward immediately. Adults frequently doom their own programs by not reinforcing immediately after the behavior is completed. Unfortunately, we sometimes expect the child to accomplish his behavior within a specified time frame, but we then hesitate in rewarding for that behavior. Arranging for dinner to be over just before a favorite television program helps to build in an immediate reward for a child's hurrying with the task of clearing the table. The reward should be offered immediately, and it should be presented contingently only on the acceptable performance of the behavior.

Item 4: Reward the behavior after it occurs. Events do not automatically arrange themselves in the correct order. Although this seems to be the most self-evident of all the items, inadvertently or deliberately disregarding it causes much of the failure of child management. As one begins to observe the *order* of events, he is struck by how frequently the arrangement is reversed. The following list illustrates this problem.

1. The student watches television *before* he starts his homework.
2. The child goes out to play *before* he picks up his room.
3. The girl calls her friend on the phone *before* she practices her piano.
4. The boy plays ball *before* he mows the lawn.

Events can be arranged to help the child accomplish desired

behaviors. Although these events occur naturally in the environment, the appropriate *arrangement* does not. Effective parenting includes arranging the events in proper sequence.

The Token Economy

The purpose of this section is to provide parents and teachers with an additional concrete, relatively simple, and easy-to-apply program which has proved to be useful in a variety of home situations. Called the "token economy," this system makes use of the behavioral principles discussed in the preceding chapter. We are referring primarily to the positive aspect of token reinforcement.

Types and Use of Tokens

Briefly, with token reinforcement, the child is given a mark or a small item as a reinforcing consequence for a specific response or pattern of responses. Stars, strips of colored paper, check marks on a tally sheet, or other small tokens signify an appropriate response or a job well done. Token reinforcers also can be poker chips, plastic bread tabs, or actual tokens. No matter what form they take, they usually are exchangeable for something of greater value. Because of this, they develop reinforcement strength for the child. Thus they can be utilized to create a workable incentive system when a lack of motivation for doing desired behavior prevails.

The use of tokens in the management of individual behavior mirrors the use of money in the general culture. That is, a type of token economy exists for our society; money is the token. Money does not satisfy any basic need, but one learns that it can be exchanged for objects which are needed or desired. Thus a child learns that money can buy candy, toys, admission to movies, and so forth. Tokens can serve the same function as money, and they are helpful in providing incentive for desirable behavior.

Tangible Positive Reinforcement

Although there is frequently a desire to reduce or weaken inappropriate behavior, the major thrust of the token economy is toward the acquisition of more useful behavior, using the principles of positive reinforcement. For many children, and particularly learning disabled ones, the social rewards typically found in many homes and classrooms just do not seem to serve as reinforcers of enough strength to perpetuate positive behavior. Consequently, the tokens underline in a concrete and tangible way the youngster's attempts toward more positive behavior. The tokens make both the desired behavior and the adult approval for that behavior obvious to the child.

Ingredients for an Effective Token Economy

There are basically five ingredients for an effective token economy program. First, behaviors to be reinforced must be identified and the contingency relationship must be clarified. Second, the reinforcement schedule must be specified. Third, social reinforcement must accompany token reinforcement. Fourth, tokens should have effective back-up reinforcers. Fifth, the child gradually should be removed from the external reinforcers. These points will be discussed in more detail.

Identifying Behaviors and Clarifying Contingency. The desired target behaviors must be clearly identified. Essentially, the adult prompts the child on the behaviors that are to be reinforced. An effective and useful way to do this is to generate a list of ways to earn tokens with the token value attached to each behavior. Those behaviors which are harder to accomplish or which are more highly valued earn more tokens. Each of the behaviors should be stated in a positive fashion. Rather than specifying "Don't hit your brother," one should list "Keep your hands to yourself when playing with your brother." In addition, identify some behaviors which are incompatible with undesirable behavior and add them to the "Ways to Earn Points" list.

Table 4 provides an illustration of one such list developed for Sally, a 10-year-old girl.

Table 4 Ways to Earn Points

Keep hands to yourself when playing with your brother (for each 15 minutes).	= 2 points
Say "please" and "thank you."	= 1 point
Pick up toys before bed.	= 1 point
Set table.	= 1 point
Play with younger sister for 30 minutes.	= 5 points
Wash dishes after dinner.	= 1 point
Make bed in morning.	= 1 point

Each of the target behaviors has been identified and stated in positive terms. The parents were attempting to encourage a more positive relationship between Sally and her four-year-old sister. Consequently, the target behaviors which would lead to this goal are given a heavier weight. That is, by not hitting and by playing with her sister, Sally could collect a large number of points. This provides excellent motivation for nonfighting behavior. A list of this kind is important because it specifically identifies target behaviors and clarifies the contingencies. It is important not to play games with the child, making him figure out what specific behavior is desired. Likewise, it is very important to make the child understand that tokens and consequently the back-up reinforcers will be awarded *only after the specified behavior has occurred.* Both adult and child should understand that rewards are *contingent.* The situation—desired behavior and contingency of rewards—should be spelled out for the child.

Specifying Reinforcement Schedule. A decision must be made on when and how often tokens will be given. Usually tokens are given to the child on the basis of a predetermined schedule, such as one token for every 15 minutes of a particular behavior (fixed interval) or one token for a certain number of times the behavior is accomplished (fixed ratio). As the behavior becomes established, it is then reinforced on a variable schedule; that is, sometimes the child achieves the token, sometimes he doesn't. In the example given above, Sally should probably be reinforced with a token *and verbal praise* each time she says "please" or "thank you." This is particularly important in the initial stages of the program. Once the polite behavior is firmly established and Sally is consistent with "please" and "thank you," she should receive a token after two polite statements, then three, then four, and so on. Eventually, Sally reaches a point where she occasionally receives a token, but the social approval supports the continuation of the polite behavior. This example represents the progression from a fixed ratio reinforcement schedule (Sally is rewarded for a set, fixed number of occurrences of a behavior: one, two, three, and so forth) to a variable reinforcement schedule.

An example of a fixed interval schedule is found in rewarding Sally for not hitting other children. This is stated in a positive way on the "Ways to Earn Points" list, and Sally is reinforced for doing a positive behavior (keeping her hands to herself) rather than being reinforced for not doing a negative behavior (don't hit others). Because she is rewarded for every fifteen minutes of doing the desirable behavior, she is said to be on an interval schedule. Initially, the token should be presented every fifteen minutes, with a gradual shift to longer periods of time required to earn the same token. Thus, as Sally is able to keep her hands to herself fairly well for fifteen minutes, the interval should increase to one token for every twenty, then every thirty minutes. Eventually, the adult increases the interval until more and more of the desired behavior is being accomplished for less and less token reward. Both of the above reinforcement schedules and, indeed, the token economy itself is designed to self-destruct.

Accompanying Tokens With Social Reinforcement. Smiles,

touching, hugs, comments, such as "Gee, you're doing well," "I feel good when you say 'thank you,'" "Keep up the good work," are absolutely critical for the success of the token economy. Social approval does two things: first, verbal and nonverbal praise and acknowledgment help increase the value of the token; second, and most important, they help realize the goal of eventually moving away from the token system so that the behavior is maintained by natural and normal reinforcers in the child's environment. The token economy program is a temporary stage in helping the child develop more desired behavior. Thus, the giving of tokens is a means by which the adult develops other rewards which will be operative in the environment so that the tokens can be dropped and the behavior maintained.

Using Effective Back-Up Reinforcers. Tokens derive their value from the child's perceiving the tokens as a viable means of exchange for other rewards that are desired. The child saves tokens until the end of a specified period—a few hours, a day, a week, or longer. At that time he turns them in for exchange for such things as candy, toys, books, games, and other rewarding objects. The Premack Principle, discussed earlier in this chapter, also can be used within the token economy by allowing the child to "buy" free time or an activity which has meaning to him. These rewards which are purchased by tokens are "back-up" reinforcers, and they can range from a single stick of gum, to an expensive toy, to a pair of shoes.

Tokens gain their reinforcing strength from the reinforcing consequences they bring. For a number of children, simply collecting the tokens reinforces and maintains desirable behavior. Their reinforcement for saving tokens may be attention from others or some other less noticeable gratification. For other children, tokens may be reinforcing only if redeemable for a desired activity or object. If the object, rate, or amount of reinforcement is not reinforcing to the child, the adult must change these elements of the program. For example, the worth of a "time token" might be increased from one-half to one hour of television time.

Providing diverse opportunities to be paid for with tokens allows for a variety of reinforcing situations. This prevents any one specific activity or object from becoming satiating to the child. Thus, tokens always remain strong reinforcers. It is wise for the adult to make a list for herself and the child of all activities, events, objects, and conditions having potential as reinforcers to the child. This list will become very extensive as the adult learns to view activities and objects in terms of their reinforcing value. Again, the adult's praise as he presents a token to the child becomes reinforcing in itself because it is paired with the reinforcement of the token.

Once a back-up reinforcement list has been developed, an appropriate price is attached to the objects and activities. Table 5 provides an example of a list which was developed for Sally. Note that the objects and activities have differing token values attached to them. A similar list can be developed by the classroom teacher for all the children in the class or for an individual child.

Table 5   Reinforcement List with Token Cost

Having a friend visit	20 points
Having a friend stay overnight	50 points
Staying overnight at a friend's	50 points
Reading time (30 minutes)	5 points
Watching television (30 minutes)	25 points
Playing with clay	10 points
Playing with vocabulary cards (30 minutes)	5 points
Getting pencils	10 points
Getting comic books	20 points
Getting felt pens	10 points
Getting combs	20 points
Using "Spill and Spell" game	20 points
Using "Scrabble" game	20 points

By utilizing such a list, Sally has a way to spend her tokens, and she becomes aware of their value. A secondary benefit of using such a list is targeting certain rewarding behaviors which are in themselves valuable to the child's development. For example, Sally can use vocabulary cards or gain reading time at very little expense to her token savings. These activities increase her verbal abilities and are much less expensive than watching television.

Removing External Reinforcers. As mentioned earlier, the child should be weaned from the external reinforcers of the token system as soon as feasible. The child must be moved to respond to reinforcements that are existent in the natural environment—most frequently social approval and praise. One easy way to begin the weaning process is to simply inflate the economy. For example, Sally would have to pay 100 tokens or points, rather than 50, to have a friend spend the night. Consequently, Sally must wait longer (or emit more of the desirable behaviors) to obtain the back-up reinforcers she wants. The adult continues to give praise and support when supplying tokens, but the child is required to delay more and more his gratification. The adult should work toward the conditions which the child will have in his environment. *That is, the token economy is truly successful only if the modification of the maladaptive behavior in the contrived environment provided by the token economy program can generalize to natural settings.*

Conclusion

The two behavioral techniques discussed in this chapter have been effective in a variety of situations. The Premack Principle provides an easy-to-use technique which can help teachers and parents in dealing with the management problems of learning disabled children. When applied appropriately, the technique is most beneficial in the home and school.

When the token system is well-designed and adequately executed, there is little doubt about its effectiveness. The dispensing of tokens provides a clear form of feedback by which the adult communicates to the child that he has done well. The use of back-up reinforcers provides great incentive for the promotion of positive behavior. The token economy establishes a more structured, and hence more predictable, environment; this outer predictability, especially for the learning disabled child, leads to an inner security. Perhaps most important of all, the token economy reminds us as adults of our need to notice and comment on the positive behaviors our children do exhibit.

PART III

PROFESSIONAL PERSPECTIVES

This section is intended primarily for school personnel who work with parents or teachers. The main theme which runs through each of these chapters is that there must be greater articulation between home and school. Learning disabled children, indeed, most children, would mature and develop more rapidly if teachers and parents cooperated more in the learning process. This section discusses the need for pupil services provided by counselors, who can carry out their commitment to children by fulfilling a consultant role.

Chapter 14 discusses the need for counseling learning disabled children and their families. Several family counseling approaches which have been used in the school are considered. Chapters 15 and 16 present several models for parent education groups. These last two chapters in particular provide a concrete structure for helping parents. Also included are suggestions on how one might use this book in advising parents.

While these chapters may be most useful to a pupil personnel worker, many teachers also might make use of this material. This may be particularly true when the school has no one to fill the role and functions of the counselor. It is important to assist parents. If the school has not provided for this service, then it often falls on the teacher to do so.

In a similar way, parents could use the following chapters as a guide to parent study groups. At the very least, parents can make use of these chapters to understand what can be done by school personnel to assist them with their child. Grass roots involvement has been a major factor in the area of learning disabilities. If parents, individually and through such groups as the American Association for Children with Learning Disabilities, had not pushed for special support, understanding, and legislation, we would not be as advanced as we are.

14

Learning Disabled Children and Their Families: A Guidance Approach

Introduction

This chapter is designed to explicate several issues important to helping the learning disabled child and his family. Emotional instability is recognized as a severe coordinate of learning disabilities. The school and the home must find ways of helping with this emotional distress. Often parents are bewildered and confused by their child's problem and need the support of the school to handle it.

In the best of all possible worlds, each elementary school would have available a school counselor to attend to the emotional and affective needs of children, including learning disabled ones. Unfortunately, this is not the best of all possible worlds, and in the interim someone—often a sensitive teacher, sometimes a principal—must respond to the issues discussed here. Material presented here is stated as if an elementary school counselor were available to implement the procedures. It is recognized that if a counselor is not available that the function must then fall upon someone else within the system.

The Assessment Process

Identifying the Disability

It is beyond the scope of this text to focus on formal assessment devices designed to identify the specific learning disability. Standardization and formal tests, such as the *Wechsler Intelligence Scale for Children* (Wechsler, 1949), the *Wide-Range Achievement Test* (Jastak and Bijou, 1946), the *Gates-McKillop Reading Diagnostic Tests* (1963), the *Peabody Picture Vocabulary Test* (Dunn, 1959), and the *Illinois Test of Psycholinguistic Abilities* (Kirk, McCarthy, and Kirk, 1968), are obviously important and must be considered in some depth for a truly accurate diagnosis of a specific learning disability.

Identifying the Learning Style

Utilizing these and other instruments as well as using informal assessment procedures, the interested adult can come to some conclusions about the child's learning deficit. This is a key concept for the teacher. Good teaching depends on good diagnosis. Diagnosis evolves through a carefully planned and executed evaluation of the child's learning.

Assessment should include seeking some understanding of the learning style of the child. De Cecco (1968) defines **learning style** as the "personal ways in which individuals process information in the course of learning new concepts and principles" (p. 75). Sperry (1973) provides a conceptual framework and a list of questions which can be used by a counselor, teacher, or parent to identify the learning style of a youngster. The most important aspect of this framework for the present discussion is the notion of identifying the primary learning, sensory modality of the learning disabled child. The three sensory modalities of greatest importance are the visual, auditory, and kinesthetic, or physical.

164

The following material is based on Sperry's (1973) excellent article. The visual modality is probably the primary learning channel of the child if he attends to, thinks about, and recalls the visual aspects of his environment. The auditory modality functions when the child remembers most vividly the music or the dialogue of an interaction. The kinesthetic modality suggests the learning conveyed through the sense of touch or movement. Recalling and re-enacting the physical properties of a movement in a situation indicate this modality.

To ascertain the dominant modality, the interested adult can observe the following: Does the child more easily remember written sources of information as being found on a particular page in a particular book (visual), or does he more easily remember jokes, discussions, or anecdotes (auditory)? Does the child focus on reading and diagrams from the blackboard (visual), or does he recall the material from lectures and discussions (auditory), or does he walk around while reading and underline the text (kinesthetic)?

In addition to observing, the counselor can identify the primary learning modality by questioning the child about a recent scene, movie, play, or television program. "What do you remember most?" and "What impressed you?" are questions that will provide useful data. Recollection of the scenery and physical descriptions of the characters suggest the visual modality. Memory of dialogue and music indicate the auditory modality. Remembering movement, texture, and choreography hint at the kinesthetic modality.

By understanding and recognizing the learning modalities utilized by the child, the adult can help him to take advantage of the strengths inherent in the dominant modality to balance his weakness. Thus by supplementing the formal and informal educational assessment of the learning disability with an informal assessment of the learning style, the adult is in a more powerful position to help the child to learn.

Counseling the Child
Encouraging the Child To Talk

One of the first steps after diagnosis of a learning disability is to talk individually with the child. Children who are learning disabled need someone with whom they can talk. The emotional, affective needs of the child are heightened by his disability. Not infrequently the child feels frustrated in the expression of his social and emotional feelings. He may tend to deny them or to bottle them up. The school, especially through the guidance function, should be seen as an agency which ameliorates rather than increases the problem. The family also should be able to provide emotional support for the child.

Guidelines for Promoting Growth and Change

In working with the learning disabled child, a great part of the counselor's (or the teacher's or the parent's) job centers around helping the child grow and change. The following suggestions are pertinent for effecting growth and change.

1. Help the child to talk about his problem. Get it out in the open where it can be discussed. Merely to be able to state a problem and discuss it may be helpful to the child.
2. Listen to the child and make him feel that you are personally interested. By receiving such attention and regard the child comes to view himself as having more potential than he thought. In many instances, an adult's listening with sympathetic understanding helps the child talk about the problem and thus modify it.
3. Identify the child's strengths and build on them. The helping adult must find some area in which the child is competent and emphasize that area. Others in the child's circle can be helped to appreciate his particular skills.

4. Isolate and specify the child's fear. If one can get the child to the specific root of his troubles, he may be able to see that he is not handicapped in all ways—only in a certain number. The isolation of fear allows for change because the child has a greater area in which to maneuver.
5. Use yourself as a corrective mirror to help the child see himself as others see him. The child needs corrective feedback in a way which cuts through the insulation. He needs to assess this data and modify himself accordingly.
6. Help the child to see that others have similar problems. By understanding that other children have difficulties, the learning disabled child can better move toward improvement. By knowing he is not uniquely bad and by seeing others succeed, the child is encouraged. This, of course, is one of the great advantages of group counseling. The discovery that others have similar problems is a great stimulus for improvement.

The child is unlikely to *immediately* change his behavior because of the preceding orientation, but he may begin to experience more self-awareness, greater self-esteem, and in effect, become less critical of himself for some of his failures. A less critical stance may help the child compensate for his shortcomings and may allow behavioral change. The counselor can assist the child in making commitments for learning activities and for social behaviors in the classroom and at home.

Helping Parents and Families

It is important for school personnel to concern themselves with the ideas, attitudes, and interrelationships existing in the child's home. It is equally important that parents understand the school's educational philosophy and processes so they can carry out the behavioral directives recommended for their child. It is for this reason that teachers and pupil personnel workers need to concern themselves with parent and family programs. The next chapter is devoted to parent educational groups which provide increased knowledge, skill, and information so that parents can make appropriate adjustments and create a better learning environment for their child. That section provides a parent and family counseling focus which is intended to facilitate a more positive expression of emotion.

Areas of Emotional Reaction

The areas of emotional reaction by parents constitute an important issue and one that needs attention by professionals. The feeling states that seem most critical are anger and hostility, guilt, and overprotection. They are briefly discussed in the following paragraphs.

Anger. The parent feels helpless and frustrated with the fact that his child has a special problem. Sometimes, the resulting hostility is expressed toward the child. Needless to say, anger expressed in this way tends to compound the problem. Sometimes, however, the anger is expressed in a blaming way so that the school, teacher, counselor, or psychologist is considered to be at fault. Obviously, this interferes with the needed cooperation between school and home. The counseling process allows parents to drain away some of the negative aspects of anger and hostility, freeing them to become more productive. The educational process allows a way of providing more of a reality base so that the inappropriate reaction may be viewed more realistically.

Guilt. The parent blames himself for the child's condition. Unfortunately, the guilt reaction usually is not effective in helping the parent improve the situation. Rather, guilt acts as a block which interferes with making changes in behavior. The guilt from past transgressions immobilizes the parent. Past behavior, even if wrong, is at least familiar. Thus the parent may fear change. New ways of behaving may create new transgressions and the parent probably feels she simply cannot tolerate any more guilt. Counseling helps the individual by catharsis. Education allows the parent to more appropriately assess responsibility for the disability. Both approaches help move the person past the guilt blockage.

Overprotection. Being indulgent and overpermissive may be an attempt to lessen feelings of guilt. The problem is that the child is prohibited from maturing in areas where he might be capable. This brings about even greater feelings of inadequacy within the child. Counseling provides the parent with a safe setting whereby his own feelings in this area can be explored and modified. This acquisition of new information may allow the person to become a more effective parenting agent.

These feelings, of course, represent only three possible reactions and are intended to be illustrative, not comprehensive. Parents of children in trouble often need counseling to help their children. Professionals are in a position to provide this help, and there are a variety of ways to proceed.

Ways To Help

Individual Parent Contact. Individual contact with parents provided by counselors, psychologists, or special teachers is an important avenue of help. These counseling sessions can help modify feelings, attitudes, and approaches which might be harmful to the child's optimal development. The individual sessions also provide parents with an understanding of their own emotional and psychological needs and help to improve the emotional climate within the family.

Counseling Groups. Parent counseling groups tend to focus on parent feelings. Although specific information about learning disabilities and emotional problems is sometimes helpful and can be provided, the main content areas for the group are the fears, hurt, anger, guilt, and frustration which are frequently experienced by parents of children with special problems.

In these groups parents are encouraged to take part in open dialogue aimed at discussing specific problems or concerns with emphasis upon emotional catharsis and the development of more effective communication patterns. The groups provide parents with an opportunity to talk over their feelings related to their own child's learning disability or behavior difficulties. One of the primary advantages of these groups is that they provide the parents with a mutual source of emotional support. Parents can relate the group experience to their own, realizing they are not alone in their fears, helplessness, and discouragement.

It is felt that one of the most important contributions of group counseling is the creation of an environment that enables parents to discuss freely their intimate feelings in many areas. The groups also provide an opportunity for the parents to develop their communication skills, enabling them to better understand and communicate with their child and with each other.

Family Group Consultation. Family group consultation combines the basic theories, methods, and advantages of both family and group counseling. The approach provides a setting in which all family members are involved in an exploration of family problems. The procedure brings several families together with two or more counselors for six to twelve sessions. A family has available the consultation services of the counseling team and other family members. Emphasis is placed on open communication among all members of the group to generate new knowledge about family interaction and new behaviors within families.

Several articles (Levine, 1966; McWhirter, 1966; Leichter and Schulman, 1972; McWhirter and Kincaid, 1974) have described the procedure as a useful *treatment* approach in helping school and clinic clients, hospital patients, and juvenile delinquents. Generally, there are three phases to the group process. The first phase is used for orientation, for an exploration of communication patterns, and for feedback among family and counseling team members about events and problems occurring in the home. It may last for 15 minutes to an hour depending on the needs of a group, and it is usually given some direction and structure by the counselor with active participation by other professionals and by family members.

In phase two, family units are broken down for either small-group or individual sessions with members of the counseling team. There is no single best formula for the structure of phase two. Parents, students, and siblings might constitute three separate small groups; likewise, parents of one family might meet with children from another family; group members with critical problems might see a counselor for an individual session. Members of the counseling team might rotate among small groups or individuals, or they might remain with one family member for several sessions to work on some specified goal.

In phase three, all members come together again in a large group to share information identified in phase two, to further explore family problems, and to set goals for family members to work on during the period between sessions.

Conclusion

With the structure provided by a parent counseling program many of the problems which confront the learning disabled child and his family can be discussed and handled. Individual parent counseling, parent group counseling, and family group consultation provide avenues to help the child's social-emotional adjustment.

15

Educational Programs
for All Parents

Introduction

This chapter and the next provide a description and outline of three educational group experiences for parents. While written primarily for use by school personnel other than classroom teachers, there is nothing that precludes a competent parent's involvement as a group leader. Teachers also could use the following models to facilitate communication, knowledge, and understanding with parents of children in their classroom. Counselors, social workers, and psychologists are in a key position to utilize the following formats because their previous training, function in the school, and emerging consultant role all lend themselves to leadership of parent groups.

The following description of parent educational groups is meant to be suggestive and to provide a model which can be adjusted according to the local situation. The groups described here are useful to parents with learning disabled children as well as parents whose children are experiencing normal adjustment problems. This chapter describes a child-management (behavior modification) group and a communication-skills group. Chapter 16 is devoted to a description of a learning disabilities group for parents. These are only a few of the potential offerings that are possible within a comprehensive parent program. Parent study groups based on Adler's and Dreikurs' ideas are common. Groups based on the concept of token economies also are quite pertinent. Then, of course, it is possible to develop groups around popular psychological and developmental ideas, such as Ginott's *Between Parent and Child* (1965), Glasser's *Reality Therapy* (1970), and Berne's Transactional Analysis (1961; 1964). Attempts should be made to determine parental needs—either by assessing them or by observing the child's reaction at school. The parent educational program then should be designed to meet these needs.

The educational groups described in this chapter were designed to function with a counselor or psychologist as the facilitator/instructor. Again, a teacher or parent with adequate understanding of the knowledge, skill, and information related to communication skills and/or behavior modification and with some sensitivity to group process could very easily serve as group leader. Eight to twelve parents constitute an optimal group size allowing opportunity for involvement of everyone and generating enough data for lively discussion. Although optimal results are found in those families where both parents participate, growth can be seen in home relationships when only one parent chooses to attend.

The sessions described here are 90 minutes long and are held every week for six weeks with an option to extend the meetings for an additional number of sessions. Mimeographed handouts and homework assignments should be used to encourage parents and to extend the impact of the group. Although texts are not absolutely necessary, it is often more productive to have these on hand for parents. The present volume has great utility in this area.

Parent Educational Group: Communication*

Parents who have children with learning disabilities and/or emotional disturbances often find that their relationship with their children has become confused and distant. Lack of communication may be at the source or a by-product of developmental difficulties. Frequently, parents want to know how to establish or regain close relationships with their children.

The purpose of this communication group is to train parents in the skills of active listening and conflict resolution. These skills are similar to those used by professionals to encourage children to discuss their problems and find practical solutions. With training, parents are better able to listen to, talk with, and aid their own children. Parental ability to communicate with children, their knowledge of how to assess problem situations, and their use of a method of problem solving not only enhance the parent-child relationship, but also teach the child to identify his feelings, explore alternatives, and take responsibility for his actions.

The following model borrows extensively from Thomas Gordon's *P.E.T.: Parent Effectiveness Training* (1970). *The Art of Helping* by Robert Carkhuff (1972) also was used. The entire course provides both the cognitive input and skill practice which parents need to begin using these techniques at home. Throughout the course, parents are encouraged to give examples from their real-life situations, and attempts are made to employ the principles of communication and problem solving to conflicts which parents are currently facing.

*Material from this section is adapted from an article by the author and Sharon E. Kahn. A parent communication group. *Elementary School Guidance and Counseling,* 9, 2, December, 1974. Chapter 10 of the present book contains additional material and information on this area and may be helpful as supplementary reading for the parent and facilitator.

Session One: Introduction
and Present Communication Patterns

The goals of the first session are to introduce the course and to help parents get acquainted. The parents also are helped to analyze their present communication patterns.

Initially, parents get acquainted by means of a warm-up exercise. They become familiar with first names and several are asked to go around the circle and name everyone present. After introductions have been made, the group leader identifies and facilitates common bonds between parents. These take the form of similarities among children, parents, problems, and feelings. For example, parents are requested to discuss problems they have in getting their children to comply with commands. This generally provides the leader with common illustrations which allow her to reflect, "I see, Mrs. Jones, that your situation is similar to Mrs. Smith's." These two procedures, getting acquainted and bonding, lead to inclusion of group members and provide links between parents which help facilitate greater communication.

To introduce the course, the group leader presents types of parents, such as winners, losers, oscillators, those who defend and exercise their power over children, those who continually give in to their children's demands, and those who find it impossible to consistently follow either an authoritarian or permissive approach. Parents are requested to share feelings they have about parental role expectations and responsibility for raising children.

The group leader diagrams on a blackboard how parental acceptance may change with different children, different situations, and a parent's current feelings. Examples are given to illustrate the flexible nature of acceptance such as: the parent who can accept his child's choice of music but does not accept that behavior if the music is played too loudly. Another example is the acceptance of many questions from the child when the parent feels rested and has lots of time and the unacceptance of that same behavior when the parent is tired and/or rushed. The importance of demonstrating acceptance is emphasized and is followed by a short discussion on the use of nonverbal acceptance, nonintervention, and passive listening.

To determine present communication patterns, parents respond to a series of representative messages from children. Responses are categorized according to Gordon's "Typical Twelve," which is a typology of typical parent responses to children's messages, such as orders, lectures, praising, blaming, and so on. The effects of these responses are then discussed. An exercise in recognizing ineffective messages concludes this session. Parents are requested to write down their responses to several hypothetical statements provided by the leader. For example, they are asked to assume that their eight-year-old son says to them, "I don't like Johnnie any more. He thinks he's big and always wants to have his way." After the parents have recorded their responses to several statements, the responses and possible effects are discussed. Blaming, for example, leads to lower self-esteem; orders build up resentments; lectures tend to cause the child to withdraw. Parents are encouraged to be aware of the messages, both verbal and nonverbal, they send to children during the coming week.

Session Two: Talking To Children

This session deals with active listening and responding to meaning. Parents are urged to share examples of how they used communication messages during the week. One parent may report having felt frustrated when she recognized that her patterns of communication were not helping her child to talk. Active listening, a skill useful in allowing a child to talk, is best used when the child owns the problem; that is, when something is disturbing to the needs of the child but does not interfere with the parent's needs (see Chapter 10). Examples of a child owning a problem include peer rejection, academic difficulties, and negative feelings about situations. Specific examples are solicited from the parents, such as little Mark's inability to get along with the other children in the neighborhood or Anna's worry about not getting her school work completed.

Ways to begin conversations are discussed. These "door openers" range from a simple "Oh" to "I'd like to hear about that."

The required attitudes, risks, and beneficial effects of listening actively and responding to implicit messages are outlined by the group leader. Also, mistakes or misuses of active listening are explored. Thus, parents are urged not to use these skills to feign interest or to manipulate the child's feelings. Parents practice identifying feelings and responding to meanings either with other parents or the group leaders in role-played situations. That is, a parent plays the role of Mark or Anna and provides the other parents with the stimulus of an actual situation to which they respond. They are encouraged to continue their practice at home. The counselor demonstrates through role play either with another counselor or with a parent how to encourage the child to talk and how to feed back the child's feelings and meaning. Carkhuff's (1972) little book, *The Art of Helping*, is particularly useful at this point.

Session Three: Sharing with Children

This session deals with sending messages to the child when the parent has a problem. Gordon (1970) suggests that the parent "owns the problem" when his or her parental needs are not being met. For example, mother "owns the problem" when she has a candy dish that she doesn't want broken. Gordon also suggests ways in which the parent can help solve the problem. Sometimes modifying or "child proofing" the environment is what is needed; that is, the dish can be put up and not used to serve candy to the child. At other times the parent may feel he must modify the child's behavior. Parents respond to role-play situations in which they must confront a child with his behavior. For example, a child may constantly interrupt his parents when they are trying to talk, or he may leave his clothing scattered about the room. One participant assumes the role and several of the parents confront the child. The effects of sending solutions or "put down" statements are outlined by the group leader. Rather than saying to the child, "you are bad because of your behavior," parents practice sending messages which emphasize their own feelings. They are encouraged to verbalize such statements as "I'm getting annoyed because you keep interrupting us" and "I'm angry at you because you don't pick up your clothes." Gordon calls this kind of message an "I-message," and he recommends that an appropriate expression of parental feelings using an "I-message" pattern greatly strengthens communication and relationships. (See Chapter 10 of this volume for more details on this type of communication.) Carkhuff's (1972) concept of confrontation is introduced in this session. Ways of communicating the discrepancy between the child's verbalizations and his behavior are considered. Parents are encouraged to restate the verbal behavior of the child (e.g., "You say that you want to help out and cooperate") and to describe the actual behavior (e.g., "and yet I have to continually pick up your clothes."). Once again, examples from home situations are solicited and role played in the group.

Session Four: Relationship Conflict

This session deals with parent-child conflicts. It is inevitable and healthy for relationships to involve problems. Parents share how they handle situations when the problem belongs to neither the child nor the parent but to the relationship; in other words, the needs of the parent conflict with the needs of the child. An example of this situation is loud talk and play by the children while Dad is

178

driving the car; another example is Mother's worry over the child's not eating adequate meals. A discussion of parental power follows, in which the counselor points out the effects of both parties battling to win. The negative aspects of the authoritarian parent are discussed as are the problems associated with the child's always getting his way. Thomas Gordon's "no-lose" method assumes that both parents and children possess relatively equal power and are capable of negotiating a solution. The "no-lose" approach requires that solutions to a problem or a conflict be acceptable to both parties; consequently, neither loses. For example, rather than yelling at the children as he drives the car, Dad and the children can discuss how the loud noise in the car leads to an unsafe driving situation. If the children are provided with comic books or simple puzzles, Dad and the youngsters can win. In a similar way, Mother and child can agree to Mother's not nagging about food if the child agrees to take a vitamin supplement.

Session Five—Conflict Resolution

This session puts into practice the "no-lose" method for resolving conflicts. Examples from the group leader and group members stress the following steps of conflict resolution:
1. Identify and define the conflict.
2. Generate possible solutions.
3. Evaluate the alternative solutions.
4. Decide on and get commitments for the best acceptable solution.
5. Work out ways of implementing the solution.
6. Follow up and evaluate how the solution worked.
Role playing by all participants is utilized to demonstrate several of the steps. Specific examples which make the steps practical and concrete are requested from parents.

Session Six—Parental Values

The goal for this session is for parents to focus on

their individual values. Parents brainstorm the variety of conflict situations they have experienced with children. Lists are drawn up of those issues that do not interfere with parental values and those which directly impose on the parent's value system. In one case, for instance, a parent may realize that whether or not his son wears long hair is a question of individual values and need not interfere with their relationship. This procedure highlights those areas wherein parents may disassociate their feelings and those issues which must be problem solved. Influencing children's values by modeling, consulting, and accepting is discussed.

Follow-up Session—Review

This session serves as a summary and review for the cognitive content of the course. The group leader reviews concepts of communication and problem solving. When available, Thomas Gordon's movie on Parent Effectiveness Training is shown.

Other areas which are attended to in this session are the general results of the training and the evaluation of the course. Parents help the group leader identify both positive and negative aspects of the program, the group interaction, and the leader's role. The leader encourages parents to formulate and share their application of new learnings and the consequent results.

Parent Educational Group: Child Management*

The child-management group is designed to impart to

* Material from this section is adapted from an article by the author and J.L. Hudak Jr. Parent's group on child management. *Devereux Forum, 10*, 1, Spring, 1975. Chapters 12 and 13 of the present book contain background information on child management techniques and should be helpful as a supplement to this educational group experience.

parents the reinforcement theory and techniques which will better equip them to deal with behaviors and misbehaviors of their children. The group process encompasses some communication skills but emphasizes reinforcement procedures. Additional input is made for handling rules in the family, and special consideration is given to individual problems, such as homework and curfew.

The principles discussed in this educational group have been derived from the behavior modification orientation. The emphasis in the group is upon making those principles useful to parents. If principles are to be practical, parents should be able to use them to cope with everyday problems of child management. The theme underlying this educational group is the notion that it is the parents, not the professional, who are the key agents of behavior change in the family. Throughout, the emphasis is upon the parent as a behavior manager. It is the parent who is primarily responsible for deciding what behaviors she wishes to change. The parent develops the understanding necessary for bringing about change. Likewise, the parent develops the skills and carries out the program which creates change.

Two texts which are useful to the leader and to the participants are *Living With Children* (1976) by Patterson and *Child Management* (1976) by Smith and Smith. Chapters 12 and 13 of the present volume also are directly applicable.

Session One—Introduction

Communication practice begins with introductory exercises in dyads, concluding with the whole group coming step-by-step to know one another. The variety of introductory experiences one uses can encourage bonding at this early stage. The exercises are chosen at the discrimination of the leader from *Awareness: Exploring, Experimenting, Experiencing* (1971) by John O. Stevens. The *Personnel and Guidance Journal*'s special issue on psychological education (Ivey and Alschuler, 1973) also describes many useful exercises.

Session Two—Positive and Negative Reinforcers

Unless additional communication exercises are continued, the initial theoretical underpinnings of reinforcement principles are introduced by the counselors in the second session. *Behaviors* and *attitudes* are differentiated and examples are elicited from group members. Positive and negative reinforcers are distinguished; punishment and bribery are distinguished from reinforcement. The complexity of several behaviors involved in a complete performance also is clarified. Homework is assigned in this session: (a) describe two acceptable behaviors and two unacceptable behaviors for each child in the home, and (b) notice the consequences following various behaviors.

Session Three—Recording Behavior

The third session begins with a sharing of homework assignment findings. The members become aware of their perceptions and their confusion of attitudes with behaviors. Parents also become aware of their own unhelpful reinforcement of negative behaviors for their children. Further instruction focuses on how to keep a record and chart of behavior and how to specifically describe behaviors. Attention is given to both frequency and duration of specific behaviors. The homework assignment is to keep a chart of one behavior of one child.

Session Four—Contingency Management

Parents share their records of behavior performance. An example is elicited in which more than one individual is involved in a behavior (e.g., sibling fighting). This is described and the counselor indicates the sequential pattern that must be broken. Instruction is given on "ignoring" child behaviors. The counselor(s) may focus on one family's behavior problem and designate the contingencies that are presently working. Other contingencies which the parents control are discussed as potential substitutes. An exemplary behavior plan is worked up with several of the parents. The parents are encouraged *not* to change their ordinary measures of control until this session.

Session Five—Consistent Reinforcement

Several experiences of parents' implementation of reinforcement procedures are discussed. Clarification of intervening variables is made and time is also given for parents to express their frustration in keeping records on reinforcement procedures. The importance of consistency of reinforcement is highlighted.

Session Six—Rules

This session utilizes the learning that has preceded. Particular application is made to handling rules as exemplified in Smith and Smith, *Child Management* (1976). A "rule" is defined as any command given by a parent to a child. The variety and multiplicity of rules used by members is elicited. Examples of inconsistency in application and enforcement are drawn out. The *sine qua non* of rules are outlined as (a) definability, (b) reasonability, and (c) enforceability. Situations involved in setting event-time limits are explained, and special situations are discussed. (This topic also may demand two sessions instead of one to give more emphasis to Smith and Smith's ideas.)

Follow-up Session

This session is intended to be an opportunity for general discussion, with parents focusing on results. Where success has occurred, the parents reinforce each other. Where difficulty has been encountered, the counselor elicits change or correction procedures from other parents and encourages their consultation abilities.

The counselor needs to arrange ways of eliciting as many parent* responses as possible. She also needs to provide the needed reinforcement to encourage parents in the development of their own strengths. Likewise, she is enabling the parents to see themselves as consultants to each other, having the resources to solve problem situations and create supportive bonds. The follow-up session may be helpful in setting the scene for other monthly meetings by the parents themselves, in which the counselor may become their professional consultant. Another potential outcome of such a group is the development of competency in parents who can lead similar groups in their own neighborhoods.

Conclusion

The old idea that parents should be encouraged to keep "hands-off" education ignores the fact that parents of children with learning disabilities carry an important key to helping their children achieve social, emotional, and educational mastery of their disabilities. By having educational experiences, such as those described, parents can better understand their children and the school program. This understanding helps build a pathway of mutual trust between the school and the parents. This link improves the educational environment of the child.

Parent educational groups offer a unique modality for increasing the school's contact with the home. They also provide an avenue whereby the parents can develop the necessary knowledge, information, and skills to more effectively rear their children. The particular skills included in these educational groups as well as the main concepts underlying a parent program have considerable relevance for the public schools, for learning disabled children, and for their parents.

16

A Program for Parents of Learning Disabled Children

Introduction

This chapter focuses on an educational experience in learning disabilities for parents. As the groups described in the previous chapter, this group also is intended to be 90 minutes long and held every week for six weeks with an option to extend the meeting time. *The use of handouts is extremely important and much of this chapter—most of the figures and tables placed at the end of the chapter—is intended for this end.* The first eight chapters of this book should prove helpful in understanding and explaining the various topics.

The underlying premise of the learning disabilities group is that increased factual knowledge tends to decrease anxiety; and, decreased anxiety permits parents to more effectively respond to their child, to the teacher, and to the child's educational experience. During the group meetings parents can be presented information and should be encouraged to discuss some of the things which bother them. Parents will discover that they are not alone; other parents have similar problems; other children have learning and behavioral problems. Generally, the aim of the group is to develop and increase parental understanding of the emotional growth and needs of the children within the context of the specific learning problems that confront the learning disabled child.

Parent Educational Group: Learning Disabilities*

The six sessions in this model are divided along the content areas of general overview and definitions, laterality and directionality, visual perception difficulties, auditory perception and discrimination problems, perceptual-motor issues, and summary and review. Two or more additional meetings are optional; they could focus on further discussion of specific learning problems with more sharing of problems related to individual youngsters. A more detailed prescription for each of the sessions follows.

Session One—Overview and Definitions

This session is begun with a presentation describing the efforts within the school to help the learning disabled child. An overview of the various facets of the state and district learning disability program is discussed, and a general outline of the parent's group on learning disabilities is presented.

Moving into the content of the session, two definitions of learning disabilities, by Kirk and Bateman (1962) and by the National Advisory Committee on Handicapped Children (1968), are provided. See Table 6 at back of chapter. Discussion is helpful in clarifying several of the concepts. Examples of child behavior are elicited to make the concepts more concrete.

*Material from this chapter is adapted with permission from an article by McWhirter, J.J. A parent education group in learning disabilities. *Journal of Learning Disabilities, 9,1*, January, 1976.

An experiential exercise is given, which requires the parents to rate three case studies in terms of how the child in each will turn out. Table 7 provides a checklist of answers and the case studies. This exercise was developed from information in the article, "Language Disabilities in Men of Eminence" (Thompson, 1971) based on Mildred and Victor Goertzel's (1962) work *Cradles of Eminence*. The cases are purported to be from the lives of Eleanor Roosevelt, Albert Einstein, and Thomas A. Edison. Those participating in the exercise should not be told this until they have completed the work. Parents are most responsive to this exercise. Although not directly related to specific learning disabilities, the case studies provide an excellent opportunity to discuss the adult adaptations to learning problems (Case 1 is Eleanor Roosevelt; Case 2 is Albert Einstein; Case 3 is Thomas A. Edison). Anderson (1970, pp. 64–69) provides additional information on this area.

Session Two—Laterality and Directionality

Definitions and examples are given for laterality and directionality. The relationship between these visual-motor skills and skills involved in reading is discussed. Information regarding these processes is found in Chapter 4.

The leader provides the experiential aspect through the use of a balance beam. Parents are asked to participate in a variety of balance beam activities including walking backward, forward, and sideways. Parents can be given a list of balance beam activities as suggested by Chaney and Kephart (1968). An adapted list of exercises is contained in Table 8 (end of chapter).

Figure 3 (end of chapter) is used to help explain to parents the learning process that Kephart (1971) has described. The "feedback mechanism" shown in this figure is discussed, and parents are asked to expand the balance exercises for their children.

Session Three—Visual Perception Problems

The input for this session is related to visual perception issues. The connections between laterality, directionality, visual perception, and reading ability are discussed.

For the experiential activity, the parents are asked to read a statement and answer questions about it. The statement simulates some of the visual perception problems which presumably face many learning disabled children. A short example of this exercise follows; a similar and more lengthy exercise is found in Chapter 4.

Isusgect th at thechil b wi tha learn ing disadility
mu stfre quent lyexger i

e

n

o

e

a

n"Alicein Won berl an b"ex is ten ce.Of ten wef in b tha the mu st co ge wi tha n unsta dlew or ib, in consistentabul ts,a nd haphaza r b gerceg tio ns.

After allowing the parents to struggle with the exercise for several minutes, the leader supplies a "correct" statement. The two short sentences above actually read:

I suspect that the child with a learning disability must frequently experience an "Alice in Wonder-land" existence. Often we find that he must cope with an unstable world, inconsistent adults, and haphazard perceptions.

Discussion focuses on the parents' frustration with the exercise. Empathy probably will be expressed toward their children, and a greater understanding of the child's learning problem likely will be achieved.

Session Four—Auditory Perception and Discrimination Problems

The close relationship between language and learning

and the role of auditory sense is emphasized in this session. Examples are given of receptive, inner, and expressive language difficulties; discussion relating to the differences between auditory *discrimination* and auditory *memory* problems occurs. This is especially interesting to the parents because of particular behavior correlations of the problems (e.g., parental injunctions such as "Take out the trash" which are not being obeyed).

A fantasy exercise is used to provide the parents with an experiential base for understanding the specific disability. Parents are asked to close their eyes and relax. A few minutes are spent in surveying the body to note any tension (see Gunther, 1968). After the parents are somewhat relaxed, the group leader asks them to focus their attention on several different sound areas (e.g., "think now about sounds within your own body; what about your breathing"). While parents are concentrating on sounds in one area, such as sound on the road outside the school room, it is pointed out that sounds within the group room, such as the clock's ticking, become less relevant. A short passage then can be read with subtle changes made in the beginning and ending sounds of words; the changes alter the meaning of the passage enough to confuse the listener.

Parallels are drawn between the exercise and the stimuli which face youngsters who have auditory perception problems. Discussion can elicit ways of disciplining and helping children with these problems. Table 9 on oral language problems (end of chapter) helps provide focus to the discussion.

Session Five—Perceptual-Motor Issues

This session is devoted to the perceptual-motor concepts of learning disabilities. Following Kephart's (1971) view of perceptual-motor development, this theory is explained as follows.

There is a progression of perceptual-motor skills that

must be developed for a child to learn at a "normal" rate. If one of these skills is not completely mastered, due to trauma, lack of stimulation, or for other reasons, higher order skills will not develop. Remediation consists of diagnosing the most basic skill not *learned* and retraining the child in perceptual-motor skills from that point.

Discussion focuses on various aspects of this theory with examples on how the theory is implemented.

Table 10 includes a list of perceptual-motor terms and a list of perceptual development exercises and remedial games. The terms and games are discussed and related to particular examples provided by the parents.

Session Six—Summary and Review

This session is used to summarize, review, and extend the concepts discussed earlier. Instances of educational procedures the school uses to help a particular child with a specific learning disability are provided.

Parents are given a list of toys that can be used to help a youngster develop certain skills (see Table 11 at end of chapter). Kephart and Radler (1960) provide further information on this point. Several games illustrative of various concepts considered in preceding meetings are demonstrated.

Sessions Seven and Eight—Optional Sessions

Additional sessions are optional. Time can be provided for a more open-ended discussion of specific problems faced by the children of attending parents. Additional ways that parents could be helpful to their children can be explored. Specific problems and techniques for helping which have been discussed during the first six sessions can become primary issues during the optional sessions.

Table 12 (back of chapter) is useful to parents in correlating learning functions with common games and tasks.

Conclusion

Parents need information about the effects of learning disabilities on their child. As parents gain more information, their understanding increases. As their understanding increases, they become potential sources of additional support for the child's learning. A parent educational group in learning disabilities is a step toward this end.

Figure 3   Diagram of Feedback Mechanism in Perception

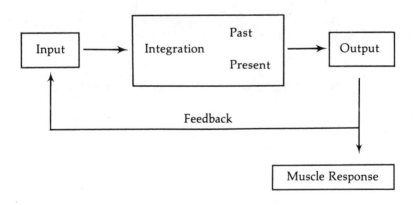

*Adapted with permission from Kephart, N.C. *The slow learner in the classroom.* 2nd Ed. Columbus: Merrill, 1971.

Table 6   Definitions of Learning Disabilities

A learning disability refers to a retardation, disorder, or delayed development in one or more of the processes of speech, language, reading, writing, arithmetic, or other school subjects resulting from a psychological handicap caused by a possible cerebral dysfunction and/or emotional or behavioral disturbances. It is not the result of mental retardation, sensory deprivation, or cultural or instructional factors. [Reprinted with permission. Kirk, S.A., and Bateman, B. Diagnosis and remediation of learning disabilities. *Exceptional Children, 29:2,* 1962, p. 73.]

The National Adivsory Committee on Handicapped Children (1968) determined that:

A learning disability refers to one or more significant deficits in essential learning processes requiring special educational techniques for its remediation.

Children with learning disability generally demonstrate a discrepancy between expected and actual achievement in one or more areas, such as spoken, read, or written language, mathematics, and spatial orientation.

The learning disability referred to is not primarily the result of sensory, motor, intellectual, or emotional handicap, or lack of opportunity to learn.

Deficits are to be defined in terms of accepted diagnostic procedures in education and psychology.

Essential learning processes are those currently referred to in behavioral science as perception, integration, and expression, either verbal or nonverbal.

Special education techniques for remediation require educational planning based on the diagnostic procedures and findings. [Reprinted with permission. National Advisory Committee on Handicapped Children. *Special Education for Handicapped Children*, First Annual Report. Washington, D.C.: U.S. Department of Health, Education, and Welfare, Office of Education, Jan. 31, 1968, p. 34.]

The reader will note the stress upon the psychological and educational aspects of learning disabilities given in these statements.

Table 7 Predicting Outcome From Case Studies*

Instructions

Read the following excerpts from case studies. Decide how each child will turn out. Indicate your decision by placing the case number in the blank which you feel appropriately describes your predicted outcome. You may choose more than one answer for each case and you may choose the same answer for more than one case. After you have made choices as an individual, discuss the cases with the whole group, helping arrive at a group decision for each case.

_____ A student (past, present, or future) in a special education classroom.

_____ A student (past, present, or future) in a resource room.

_____ Will outgrow difficulties.

_____ Will not outgrow difficulties without psychological or psychiatric help.

_____ Will be mentally deficient.

_____ Will be gifted.

_____ Will be psychotic and need to be institutionalized.

_____ Will be delinquent.

_____ Will be neurotic but otherwise adjust to conditions without being institutionalized.

_____ A learning disabled child (past, present, or future).

_____ An emotionally disturbed child (past, present, or future).

_____ The child will be beyond the help of school personnel.

*Material adapted with permission. Goertzel, V., and Goertzel, M. *Cradles of Eminence*. Boston: Little, Brown, 1962.

Case 1. Girl, at age 16, orphaned, willed to custody of grandmother, who was separated from alcoholic husband, now deceased. The mother rejected the homely child, who was proved to lie and steal sweets. Girl swallowed a penny to attract attention at age 5. Father was fond of child. Child lived in fantasy as the mistress of father's household for years. Four young uncles and aunts in household could not be managed by grandmother. Young uncle drank, had love affair, and locked himself in room. Grandmother resolved to be more strict with children. She dressed granddaughter oddly, refused to let her have playmates, and put her in braces to keep her back straight. Did not send her to grade school. Aunt on paternal side of family crippled; uncle asthmatic. How will this child turn out?

Case 2. Boy, senior year of high school, has obtained ceritificates from physician stating that nervous breakdown makes it necessary for him to leave school for six months. Boy not a good all-around student; has no friends. Teachers find him a problem; he started talking at a late age. Father was ashamed of son's lack of athletic ability and poor adjustment to school. Boy has mannerisms, makes up own religion, chants hymns to himself. Parents regard him as "different." How will this child turn out?

Case 3. Boy, age six, had large head at birth. Thought to have had brain fever. Three siblings died before his birth. Mother does not agree with relatives and neighbors that child is probably abnormal. Child sent to school and was diagnosed as mentally ill by teacher. Mother is angry and withdraws child from school; says she will teach him herself. How will this child turn out?

Table 8   Balance Beam Exercises*

1. Walk forward on beam, arms held sideward to help balance. Repeat, backward.
2. With arms held sideward, walk to the middle, turn around, and walk backward.
3. Walk forward to the middle of the beam, turn, and walk the remaining distance sideways to left with weight on the balls of the feet.
4. Walk to center of beam, turn, and continue sideways to right.
5. Walk forward with left foot always in front of right. Repeat, backward.
6. Walk forward with right foot always in front of left. Repeat, backward.
7. Walk forward with hands on hips. Repeat, backward.
8. Walk forward and pick up a chalk eraser from the middle of the beam.
9. Walk forward to center, kneel on one knee, rise, and continue to end of beam.
10. Walk forward with eraser balanced on top of head. Repeat, backward.
11. Place eraser at center of beam. Walk to center, place eraser on top of head, continue to end of beam.
12. Have partners hold a wand 12 inches above the center of the beam. Walk forward on beam and step over the wand.
13. With wand still held 12 inches above beam, walk backward and step over wand.
14. Hold wand at height of 4 feet. Walk forward and pass under it. Repeat, backward.
15. Walk the beam backward with hands clasped behind the body.

*Adapted from Chaney, A.B. and Kephart, N. C. *Motoric aids to perceptual training*. Columbus: Merrill, 1968.

16. Walk the beam forward, arms held sideward, palms down, with an eraser on the back of each hand. Repeat, backward.
17. Walk the beam forward, arms held sideward, palms up, with an eraser on the palm of each hand. Repeat, backward.
18. Walk the beam sideward to right, with weight on balls of feet. Repeat, except go to left.
19. Walk forward to middle of beam, kneel on one knee, straighten the right leg forward until heel is on the beam and knee is straight. Rise and walk to end of beam. Repeat, left leg.
20. Walk backward to middle of beam. Kneel on one knee, straighten right leg forward until heel is on the beam and knee is straight. Rise and walk to end of beam. Repeat, left leg.
21. Hop on right foot the full length of beam. Repeat, left foot.
22. Hop on right foot the full length of beam, turn around, and hop back. Repeat, left foot.
23. Walk to middle of beam, balance on one foot, turn around on this foot, and walk backward to end of beam.
24. With arms clasped about body in rear, walk the beam forward. Repeat, backward.

Table 9   Oral Language Problems*

Oral aspects of language are unique to man and are one of man's greatest achievements. The close relationship between language and learning is extremely important. Children with oral language problems are handicapped in understanding and using the spoken word. Consequently, difficulties in acquiring basic academic skills also are observed in many individual cases.

Deficits in oral language can be very complex. A speech clinician should be consulted for guidance and assistance in helping children with significant language deficits. The development of oral language skills must be recognized as an important goal which the concerned adult helps the child achieve. One must be aware of the three basic aspects of language acquisition and the difficulties usually associated with each of them.

Receptive Language Difficulties. Receptive language is the ability to understand the spoken language of others. The child with difficulties in this area hears what is said but is unable to understand it. Adequate receptive language involves the ability to:
1. Auditorally perceive sounds.
2. Understand concrete and abstract words.
3. Understand the linguistic structure of sentences.
4. Follow directions.
5. Listen critically and make judgments.

Inner Language Difficulties. Inner language can be defined as the language which one uses to communicate with oneself or the language with which one thinks. Inner language disorders are the most complex of all language difficulties. Inner language development is dependent upon the child's ability to:

*Adapted with permission. Wallace, G., and Kauffman, J.M. *Teaching children with learning problems.* Columbus: Merrill, 1973.

1. Establish verbal imagery for sounds, words, and concepts.
2. Use the skills needed in a logical thinking process.

Expressive Language Difficulties. Expressive language is the spoken language the child uses in communication with others. Adequate expressive language is dependent upon acquiring meaningful units of experience and establishing comprehension. In addition, the child must be able to:

1. Produce various speech sounds.
2. Formulate words and sentences and exhibit adequate vocabulary.
3. Use correct grammatical and syntactical language patterns.

Table 10   Perceptual-Motor Concepts (Terms)

Posture. A dynamic, shifting control of one's body, which to be "good" should be loose, flexible, and comfortable. Balance.

Kinesthetic. Pertaining to "the knowledge of muscles"; i.e., the sense or perception gained from the feelings created by one's own movements and bodily tensions.

Laterality. Awareness of left and right, etc., within one's own body; also differentiation between one's left and right side; also, differentiation of top-bottom, back-front. Dominance (develops around two years).

Directionality. Awareness of left-right, front-back, up-down, etc., in the world around the self.

Egocentric localization. The earliest form of space awareness in which the position of any person or object is defined in relation to one's self.

Objective localization. Perceiving the positioning of objects in space in relation to one another.

Globular form. Overall perception of an object without viewing its details and without understanding how the object is put together.

Integrated form. Detailed and accurate perception of an object including awareness of how the parts of the object go together to make a complete whole.

Reading readiness. Preparedness to learn to read, based upon the previous learning of numerous psychomotor, postural, and perceptual skills.

Perceptual Development Exercises
and/or Remedial Games

1. Angels in the snow
   Develops muscular control, body awareness, timing and coordination.
2. Walking and balance board
   Teaches balance, postural response, and right-left directionality.
3. Drawing games
   Involves directionality and translation of tactual and kinesthetic information into vision.
4. Pegboard games
   Contributes to improved laterality and directionality.
5. Ball games
   Involves egocentric localization and objective localization and spatial relationships.

Table 11   Toys That Teach*

Gross motor skills:
    Balls, variety: soft ball, tennis, hard ball
    Stilts
    Hula hoops
    Jump rope
    Ring-toss set
    Pogo stick

Self-identification:
    Full-length mirror
    Scrapbook and paste
    Camera
    Models of detailed body parts: The Beating Heart,
        The Seeing Eye, The Human Brain, The Visible
        Man, The Visible Woman
    Human body kit
    Doll house and materials

Balance and rhythm:
    Balance boards
    Jumping board
    Climbing rope
    Skateboard
    Bicycle

Manual dexterity:
    Peg board
    Tinker toys
    Model cars, boats, airplanes
    Assorted nuts and bolts for sorting tasks
    Erector set

*Adapted with permission. Irma Letson, Teacher and Co-ordinator, Clinic Classroom, Devereux Day School, Scottsdale, Arizona, 1973. (Mimeographed.)

Tactile discrimination:
   Sandbox
   Fingerpaint
   Clay
   Scissors and cutting materials
   Felt pens and drawing paper

Laterality:
   Punching bag
   Balance beam
   Jump rope

Auditory-vocal association:
   Walkie-talkie
   Real telephone
   Dr. Seuss books
   Radio
   Talking books
   Tape recorder

Visual acuity:
   Microscope
   Telescope
   Large prism
   Viewmaster

Visual coordination and pursuit:
   Moving target toy gun set
   Balloons
   Penlight, flashlight
   Ping-pong set

Visual-motor fine muscle coordination:
   Pick-up sticks
   Marble games
   Etch-a-Sketch
   Paint-by-number sets
   Activity books: follow the dots
   Yo-yo

Table 11   (cont.)

Interlocking cubes:
> Building blocks
> Geometric solid blocks
> Farm set and three-dimensional animals
> Varied puzzles
> Jacks and ball set
> Large beads and laces
> Weaving and loom sets or kits
> Bingo games

General:
> Records of stories and songs
> Checkers
> Dominoes
> Playing cards
> Barrel of Monkeys
> Shape-O by Tupperware
> Play-doh
> Crayons
> Soft pencils
> Newsprint, plain
> Fingerpaints
> Magnetic alphabet board
> Hammer, nails, boards
> Hand puppets

Table 12   Teaching Materials as an Aid to Learning

	Classification	Directionality	Eye-Hand Coordination	Fine Muscle Development	Form Discrimination	Increased Attention Span	Laterality	Left-to-Right Progression	Limitation of Perseveration	Spatial Relationships
Block design		x	x	x		x		x	x	x
Coding		x	x	x		x		x		x
Cutting			x	x	x	x	x			x
Matching	x	x	x			x	x	x	x	
Parquetry			x		x	x				
Peg boards		x	x	x	x	x	x	x	x	x
Puzzles		x	x		x	x				x
Scan	x	x	x	x	x	x		x	x	x
Sew-ons by Colorforms			x	x	x	x	x		x	x
Sorting	x	x	x	x		x			x	

Epilogue
Déjà Vu

Once there was a child named Mark—a very loved child who was much wanted by his mother, father, and older brothers and sister. He was born and developed in a nonremarkable way, apparently happy and apparently "normal." There were only hints at future problems. When Mark set the table for his mother, sometimes the placemats were placed upside down and since the placemats were cut-out animal figures, it did look strange to have an upside-down elephant lying in front of you. But, of course, all children make mistakes like that. Don't they?

When Mark started school, some of his teachers were helpful and kind and supportive; some were impatient, critical, and self-centered. Kindergarten was not a good year, but first grade was better. Mark didn't have a lot of written work and often didn't bring anything home. On occasion the teacher would complain about a short attention span, even though Mark sat and worked on his papers long after the other children were at play. Mark's parents began to suspect a learning disability. But there are such things as developmental lags, and a lot of children show improvement naturally as the year goes on. And we do start boys to school too early; they usually grow out of it.

Then came the second grade. "Learning disabilities" are well publicized. Arizona has a mandate to educate all exceptional children. Federal legislation has progressed; some teachers and some parents recognize the manifestations of learning disabilities.

For a Halloween assignment Mark did the work seen in Figure 4 (page 208).

Translated and reversed, the sentences read:

> P is for Pumpkin
> G is for Ghost
> W is for Witch
> S is for Skeleton.

If the teacher did not recognize problems here, Mark's parents did. And developmental lag or not, testing was requested. There was considerable delay.

——Mark is such a quiet, well-behaved boy, the ones that really need testing in here are the noisy ones.

——We've tested the quota this semester in this school. The school psychologist is too busy.

——Why doesn't his father (a psychologist) test Mark himself? Or perhaps have him tested?

Finally, after much delay, testing was done. The results: learning disability—visual perception problems with reversal of images (the elephants and "nikpump" told us that) and auditory memory difficulties (so that's one reason why he sometimes "forgets" to take out the garbage).

The testing resulted in a meeting with parents, principal, counselor, psychologist, and several teachers. From this meeting came an educational plan: Provide regular classroom involvement with several hours a day in the resource room to work on the specific learning deficit. Teach new material in the sense modality most developed. Remediate the areas of deficiency.

Figure 4 The Work of Mark, a Learning Disabled Child

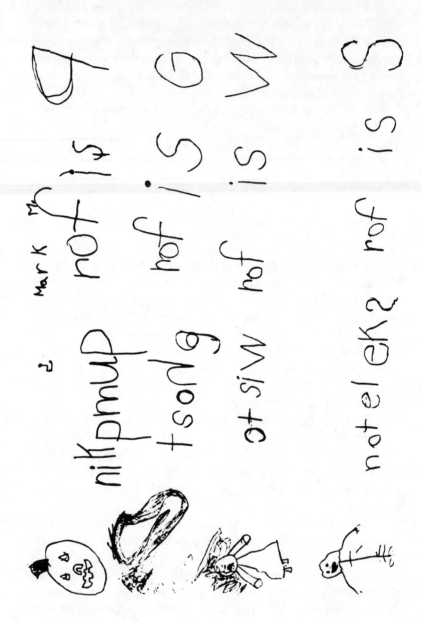

The plan is in effect; the prognosis good. After one year, most of the reversals have been eliminated, and Mark's memory is improving.

The reader recognizes, of course, that Mark is my son. He is the fourth of my five children and the second child to have a learning disability severe enough to limit his ability to learn educational material. My responses now and my responses several years ago are interesting.

I'm still saddened and frustrated when I think of the difficulties which face Mark in the learning process. But on the whole, I'm optimistic. My optimism is based on several factors.

First, in the process of thinking, discussing, reading, and finally writing this book, Mary and I have learned a great deal. This knowledge gives a sense of security and support. It also gives confidence that we can help psychologically in the communication, structure, and support we provide for the children. We also can help educationally in the games, activities, and exercises we engage Mark in. If we can learn to help, other parents also can learn to help.

Second, Mark himself and his brothers and sisters have a greater understanding of learning disabilities and the stresses they create. This understanding gives all of us better control and power. Maybe, just maybe, all of us are a little more tolerant and accepting of individual differences (although in Mom and Dad's case, maybe it's that we're just a little bit older and a little bit more tired). Other families can become more flexible also.

Third, school people are more aware of learning disabilities and apparently more willing to respond to special problems. When we determined Bob's problem, there were no resources for the learning disabled child in the public schools. We were forced to enroll him in a private summer school and to seek out a tutor to work with him and with us. Five years later, Mark has a resource room and a special reading teacher available to him as a part of the public school curriculum. The number of school psychologists and elementary school counselors has also increased. Many public schools have shown great improvement in the learning disabilities area, at least in the past several years.

Fourth, I have come to believe that success is not based on the easy way, that the process of life is a struggle, and that greater struggle potentially leads to greater success. Consider the following which demonstrates the struggles of some important people:*

Einstein was four years old before he could speak and seven before he could read. *Issac Newton* did poorly in grade school, and *Beethoven's* music teacher once said of him, "As a composer he is hopeless." When *Thomas Edison* was a boy, his teachers told him he was too stupid to learn anything. *F.W. Woolworth* got a job in a dry goods store when he was 21, but his employers would not let him wait on a customer because he "didn't have enough sense." A newspaper editor fired *Walt Disney* because he had "no good ideas." *Caruso's* music teacher told him, "You can't sing. You have no voice at all." *Abraham Lincoln* entered the Black Hawk War as a captain and came out as a private. *Louisa May Alcott* was told by an editor that she could never write anything that had popular appeal. *Winston Churchill* failed the sixth grade in school.

Probably these people were identified as low achievers in school or as misfits on their job or as "retards" by their peers. Even (or, perhaps, especially) the successful have known stress and defeat. We need to find ways to help our learning disabled develop their own success.

Finally, I'm optimistic because Bob (the Robert of Chapter 1) is making good progress. At the time of publication, he is a high school sophomore. Some subjects

*Published with permission. Larson, Milton E. Humbling cases for career counselors. *Phi Delta Kappan*, Feb. 1973, p. 374.

are much harder than others, but he can compensate. Indeed, in some areas he excels because he has compensated so much.

He overhears conversations about finishing a table in cork and when the statement is "Wood would click and cork cushions the glass," he *hears* "Woodwin was caught pushing the grass." Our knowing that auditory discrimination is a problem allows all of us the freedom to laugh and to clarify.

Bob doesn't play baseball because fine-muscle coordination is still a problem, so he competes in track instead. He is a fine rebounder in basketball but doesn't shoot too well.

He is continuing to learn to feel good about himself, but aren't we all still doing that.

Some high school teachers are understanding and tolerant of individual differences; others are still teaching a subject and not youngsters. Some seem unknowledgeable about learning disabilities and perhaps need more information concerning this problem at the high school level. But that's another book.

References

Anderson, R.P. *The child with learning disabilities and guidance.* Boston: Houghton Mifflin, 1970.

Balow, B. Perceptual-motor activities in the treatment of severe reading disabilities. *The Reading Teacher,* 24: 513-525, Mar., 1971.

Bandura, A. *Principles of behavior modification.* New York: Holt, Rinehart, and Winston, 1969.

Bannatyne, A. Diagnosis and remedial techniques for use with dyslexia children. *Academic Therapy Quarterly, 3, 4,* Summer, 1968, p. 218.

Bannatyne, A. *Language, reading and learning disabilities.* Springfield, Ill.: Charles C. Thomas, 1971.

Bannatyne, A.; Chaney, A.B.; and Kephart, N.C. *Motoric aids to perceptual training.* Columbus: Merrill, 1968.

Barry, H. *The young aphasic child: Evaluation and training.* Washington, D.C.: Alexander Graham Bell Association for the Deaf, 1961.

Barsch, R.H. *A movigenic curriculum.* Madison, Wis.: State Department of Public Instruction, 1965.

Barsch, R.H. *Achieving perceptual-motor efficiency: A space-oriented approach to learning.* Seattle: Special Child Publications, 1967.

Becker, W.C. *Parents are teachers: A child management program.* Champaign, Ill.: Research Press, 1971.

Berne, E. *Transactional analysis in psychotherapy.* New York: Grove Press, 1961.

Berne, E. *Games people play.* New York: Grove Press, 1964.

Bettelheim, B. *Love is not enough: The treatment of emotionally disturbed children.* Glencoe, Ill.: Free Press, 1950.

Block, J.H., and Anderson, L.W. *Mastery learning in classroom instruction.* New York: MacMillan, 1975.

Carkhuff, R.R. *The art of helping.* Amherst, Mass.: Human Resources Development Press, 1972.

Chaney, A.B., and Kephart, N.C. *Motoric aids to perceptual training.* Columbus: Merrill, 1968.

Chomsky, N. *Syntactic structures.* The Hague: Mouton, 1957.

Cruickshank, W.M. *A teaching method for brain-injured and hyperactive children.* Syracuse, N.Y.: Syracuse University Press, 1961.

Cruickshank, W.M. *The brain-injured child in home, school, and community.* Syracuse, N.Y.: Syracuse University Press, 1967.

De Cecco, J. *The psychology of learning and instruction.* Englewood Cliffs, N.J.: Prentice-Hall, 1968.

Delacato, C.H. *The treatment and prevention of reading problems.* Springfield, Ill.: Thomas, 1959.

Delacato, C.H. *The diagnosis and treatment of speech and reading problems.* Springfield, Ill.: Thomas, 1963.

Delacato, C.H. *Neurological organization and reading.* Springfield, Ill.: Thomas, 1966.

Dinkmeyer, D., and Dreikurs, R. *Encouraging children to learn: The encouragement process.* Englewood Cliffs, N.J.: Prentice-Hall, 1963.

Dreikurs, R. *Psychology in the classroom.* New York: Harper and Row, 1957.

Dreikurs, R. *The challenge of parenthood.* Rev. ed. New York: Sloan and Pearce, 1958.

Dreikurs, R. *Children: The challenge.* New York: Hawthorne, 1964.

Dreikurs, R., and Grey, L. *A parents' guide to child discipline.* New York: Hawthorne, 1970.

Dreikurs, R.; Grunwald, B.B.; and Pepper, F.C. *Maintaining sanity in the classroom.* New York: Harper and Row, 1971.

Drew, A.L. A neurological appraisal of familial congenital word-blindness. *Brain, 79,* 440-460, 1956.

Dunn, L.M. *Peabody Picture Vocabulary Test.* Minneapolis: American Guidance Service, 1959.

Dunn, L.M.; Smith, J.O.; and Horton, K.B. *Peabody language development kits,* Level I and Level II. Minneapolis: American Guidance Service, 1965.

Felker, D.W. *Building positive self-concepts.* Minneapolis: Burgess, 1974.

Fernald, G.M. *Remedial techniques in basic school subjects.* New York: McGraw-Hill, 1943.

Frostig, M., and Horne, D. *The Frostig program for the development of visual perception: Teacher's guide.* Chicago: Follett, 1964.

Frostig, M.; Maslow, P.; Lefever, D.W.; and Whittlesey, J.R.B. *The Marianne Frostig Developmental Test of Visual Perception, 1963 standardization.* Palo Alto, Calif.: Consulting Psychologist, 1964.

Gates, A.I., and McKillop, A.S. *Gates-McKillop Reading Diagnostic Tests.* New York: Bureau of Publications, Teachers College, Columbia University, 1963.

Getman, G.N. Visual success in reading success. *Journal of the California Optometric Association, 29* (5), 1-4, 1961.

Getman, G.N. *How to develop your child's intelligence.* Luverne, Minn.: G.N. Getman, 1962.

Getman, G.N., and Hendrickson, H.H. The needs of teachers for specialized information on the development of visual-motor skills in relation to academic performance. In W.M. Cruickshank, ed., *The teacher of brain-injured children.* Syracuse: Syracuse University Press, 1966.

Getman, G.N.; Kane, E.R.; Halgren, M.R.; and McKee, G.W. *Developing learning readiness.* Manchester, Mo.: McGraw-Hill, Webster Division, 1968.

Ginott, H.G. *Between parent and child.* New York: Avon Books, 1965.

Glasser, R. *Reality therapy.* New York: Harper and Row, 1970.

Goertzel, V., and Goertzel, M. *Cradles of eminence.* Boston: Little, Brown, 1962.

Gordon, T. *P.E.T.: Parent effectiveness training.* New York: Peter H. Wyden, 1970.

Gunther, B. *Sense relaxation.* New York: Collier-Macmillan, 1968.

Hardy, W. Problems of audition, perception, and understanding. *Volta Review*, June, *68*, 1956.

Hartman, A.S. *Preschool Diagnostic Language Program.* Harrisburg, Pa.: Department of Public Instruction, 1966.

Heber, R. Modifications in the manual on terminology and classifications in mental retardation. *American Journal of Mental Deficiency, 46*, 1961.

Hermann, K. *Reading disability.* Springfield, Ill.: Thomas, 1959.

Homme, L.E. Human motivation and environment. *Kansas Studies in Education*, Lawrence, Kansas, *16*, 1966.

Ivey, A.E., and Alschuler, A.S., eds. Psychological education: A prime function of the counselor. *Personnel and Guidance Journal, 51*, 9, May, 1973.

Jakobson, R. *Child language. Aphasia and phonological universals.* The Hague: Mouton, 1968.

Jastak, J., and Bijou, S. *Wide Range Achievement Test.* New York: Psychological Corporation, 1946.

Johnson, D.J., and Myklebust, H.R. *Learning disabilities: Educational principles and practices.* New York: Grune and Stratton, 1964.

Kephart, N.C. *The slow learner in the classroom.* 2nd ed. Columbus: Merrill, 1971.

Kephart, N.C., and Radler, D.H. *Success through play.* New York: Harper and Brothers, 1960.

Kirk, S.A. *The diagnosis and remediation of psycholinguistic disabilities.* Urbana: University of Illinois Press, 1966.

Kirk, S.A. *Educating exceptional children.* Boston: Houghton Mifflin, 1972.

Kirk, S.A., and Batemen, B. Diagnosis and remediation of learning disabilities. *Exceptional Children, 29*, 2, 1962.

Kirk, S.A.; McCarthy, J.J.; and Kirk, W.D. *Illinois Test of Psycholinguistic Abilities. Rev. ed. Examiner's Manual.* Urbana: University of Illinois Press, 1968.

Kirshner, A.J. *Training that makes sense.* San Rafael, Calif.: Academic Therapy Publications, 1972.

Krumboltz, J.D., and Krumboltz, H.B. *Changing children's behavior.* Englewood Cliffs, N.J.: Prentice-Hall, 1972.

Krumboltz, J.D., and Thoresen, C.E. *Behavioral counseling: Cases and techniques.* New York: Holt, Rinehart, and Winston, 1969.

Langford, W.S., and Olson, E. Clinical work with parents of child patients. In Noland, R.L., ed., *Counseling parents of emotionally disturbed children.* Springfield, Ill.: Thomas, 1972.

Larson, Milton E. Humbling cases for career counselors. *Phi Delta Kappan,* 374, Feb., 1973.

Leichter, E., and Schulman, G.L. Interplay of group and family treatment techniques in multifamily group therapy. *International Journal of Group Psychotherapy, 22,* 167-176, 1972.

Lenneberg, E. *New directions in the study of language.* Cambridge: MIT Press, 1964.

Letson, I. Unpublished resource. Devereux Day School and Clinic, Scottsdale, Arizona, 1973.

Levine, E. Therapeutic multiple family groups. *International Journal of Group Psychotherapy, 16,* 203-208, 1966.

Lewis, R.S. *The other child.* New York: Grune and Stratton, 1951.

McCarthy, J.J., and McCarthy, J.F. *Learning disabilities.* Boston: Allyn and Bacon, 1969.

McGinnis, M.A. *Aphasic children.* Washington, D.C.: Volta Bureau, 1963.

McWhirter, J.J. Family group consultation and the secondary schools. *Family Life Coordinator, 15, 1966.*

McWhirter, J.J. A parent education group in learning disabilities. *Journal of Learning Disabilities, 9,* 1, Jan., 1976.

McWhirter, J.J., and Hudak, J.L. Parent's group on child-management. *Devereux Forum, 10,* 1, Spring, 1975.

McWhirter, J.J., and Kahn, S.E. A parent communication group. *Elementary School Guidance and Counseling, 9, 2,* Dec., 1974.

McWhirter, J.J., and Kincaid, M. Family group consultation: Adjunct to a parent program. *Journal of Family Counseling, 1, 2,* 45-48, 1974.

Maw, W.H., and Maw, E.W. Self-concepts of high- and low-curiosity boys. *Child development, 41,* 123-129, 1970.

Meyers, P.I., and Hammill, D.D. *Methods for learning disorders.* New York: Wiley, 1969.

Myklebust, H.R. *The psychology of deafness: Sensory deprivation, learning and adjustments.* New York: Grune and Stratton, 1960.

National Advisory Committee on Handicapped Children. *Special Education for Handicapped Children,* First Annual Report. Washington, D.C.: U.S. Department of Health, Education, and Welfare, Office of Education, Jan. 31, 1968.

Patterson, G.R. *Families: Applications of social learning to family life.* Champaign, Ill.: Research Press, 1975.

Patterson, G.R. *Living with children.* Champaign, Ill.: Research Press, 1976.

Penfield, W., and Roberts, L. *Speech and brain mechanisms.* Princeton, N.J.: Princeton University Press, 1959.

Premack, D. Reinforcement theory. In D. Levin, ed., *Nebraska Symposium on Motivation: 1965*. Lincoln, Neb.: University of Nebraska Press, 1965.

Reger, R.; Schroeder, W.; and Uschold, K. *Special education: Children with learning problems*. New York: Oxford University Press, 1968.

Rogers, C.R. *On becoming a person*. Boston: Houghton Mifflin, 1961.

Rogers, C.R., and Stevens, B. *Person to person: The problem of being human*. New York: Pocket Books, 1971.

Shaw, M.C., and Alves, G.J. The self-concept of bright academic underachievers: II. *Personnel and Guidance Journal*, 42, 401-403, 1963.

Skinner, B.F. *Science and human behavior*. New York: Macmillian, 1953.

Skinner, B.F. *Beyond freedom and dignity*. New York: Knopf, 1971.

Smith, J.M., and Smith, D.E.P. *Child management*. Champaign, Ill.: Research Press, 1976.

Sommers, R.K., and Brady, D. *A manual of speech training methods using the echorder*. South Ampton, Pa.: RIL Electrons, 1964.

Sperry, L. Counselors and learning style. *Personnel and Guidance Journal*, 51, 7, 478-483, 1973.

Stevens, John O. *Awareness: Exploring, experimenting, experiencing*. Lafayette, Calif.: Real People Press, 1971.

Strauss, A.A., and Kephart, N. *Psychopathology and education of the brain-injured child, Vol. 2*, New York: Grune and Stratton, 1955.

Terman, L.M., and Merrill, M. *Revised Stanford-Binet Intelligence Testing*. Chicago: Education-Industry Service, 1960.

Thompson, L.J. Language disabilities in men of eminence. *Journal of Learning Disabilities, 4*, 1, Jan., 1971.

Vergason, G.A. Facilitation of memory in the retardate. *Exceptional Children, 34*, 1968.

Wallace, G., and Kauffman, J.M. *Teaching children with learning problems.* Columbus: Merrill, 1973.

Wechsler, D. *Wechsler Intelligence Scale for Children.* New York: The Psychological Corporation, 1949.

Wepman, J. *Auditory Discrimination Test.* Chicago: Language Research Associates, 1958.

Wepman, J., and Jones, L. *Studies in aphasia: An approach to testing.* Chicago: Education-Industry Service, 1961.

Wiseman, D.E. A classroom procedure for identifying and remediating language problems. *Mental Retardation, 3*, 20-24, 1965.